TEEN SUICIDE
Too Young to Die

Cynthia Copeland Lewis

—Issues in Focus—

ENSLOW PUBLISHERS, INC.
Bloy St. and Ramsey Ave.   P.O. Box 38
Box 777   Aldershot
Hillside, N.J. 07205   Hants GU12 6BP
U.S.A.   U.K.

Copyright © 1994 by Cynthia Copeland Lewis

Library of Congress Cataloging-in-Publication Data

Lewis, Cynthia Copeland, 1960–
    Teen suicide: too young to die / Cynthia Copeland Lewis.
        p. cm. — (Issues in focus)
    Includes index.
    Summary: Describes the problems that can lead to suicide and ways
to prevent it, with true stories to illustrate the issues under
discussion.
    ISBN 0-89490-433-7
    1. Teenagers—United States—Suicidal behavior—Juvenile
literature. 2. Suicide—United States—Prevention—Juvenile
literature. [1. Suicide.] I. Title. II. Series: Issues in focus
(Hillside, N.J.)
HV6546.L49 1994
362.2'8'0835—dc20   93-25010
                                                         CIP
                                                            AC

Printed in the United States of America

10 9 8 7 6 5 4 3 2

Cover Illustration: © Stuart Simons, 1993

Acknowledgement

The author and publisher would like to thank the following reviewers and advisors for their invaluable insight and many helpful suggestions:

"I have reviewed the information presented in this book and find it to be accurate."
  —Alan L. Berman, Ph.D.
    Director
    National Center for the Study
    and Prevention of Suicide
    Washington School of Psychiatry

"I find this book to be accurate and informative."
  —Toni DeMarco, MFCC
    Director
    Youth Outreach Services at the Crisis
    Intervention and Suicide Prevention Center of
    San Mateo County

Dedication

For Bob and Gail, parents of Michelle
For Mary and Frank, parents of Brian
For Roger, father of Jennifer
For Dan, brother of Jennifer
For Lois, grandmother of Jennifer
. . . and for the thousands of others who are struggling to cope with the loss of a loved one to suicide.

Contents

Part I What Is Suicide?   6

  1 Michelle's Story   7

  2 An Overview   14

Part II Why?   26

  3 The Suicidal Individual   27

  4 Suicide and the Family   44

  5 Suicide and Society   60

Part III Prevention   74

  6 Helping a Friend   75

  7 Helping the Cause   85

  8 Helping Yourself   93

Part IV Afterwards   105

  9 Coping in the Aftermath of Suicide   106

Part V Lost Potential   120

  10 What Did the Future Hold?   121

Resources   124

Further Reading   126

Index   127

Part I

What Is Suicide?

Newspapers shock readers with headlines. Reports show bar graphs and offer lists of data about suicides. Researchers study surveys and medical examiners' notes and then write papers on the subject. But all of this information, important as it may be, does not tell us about the human side of suicide: the pain of the victim, the grief and the guilt of the survivors. Five thousand young people complete suicide every year. In the first chapter, you will read about one of these suicides, Michelle's, as told to me by her parents.

In Chapter 2, you will learn about the scope of the problem: the number of young people who take their own lives, the number who make an attempt, the differences between male and female suicides, and the role drugs and alcohol play in teen suicide. Our greatest weapon in the war on youth suicide is education. The more we understand about suicide, our enemy, the better able we are to plan our defenses.

1

Michelle's Story

Michelle was born on August 15, 1966. Her parents joyfully announced the arrival of their first child. Baby Michelle got her first tooth when she was seven months old.

When Michelle was two, her mother gave her a lopsided haircut and wept at the results.

Photographs of Michelle's third Christmas show her delighted reaction to the child-size kitchen from Santa. Her stocking was pinned to a brightly colored, cardboard fireplace that was set up every Christmas because the house they lived in didn't have a real fireplace.

She got her second haircut when she was 4—this time, at a beauty parlor.

On her fifth birthday, she blew out the candles on a cake shaped like a little girl. Perhaps she wished for a baby sister because, two weeks later, she got one.

She joined the Girl Scouts when she was about eight, and her mother helped out as a leader. Camping had always been a favorite family activity.

The Christmas Michelle was 10, her father asked her and her sister Jenny to select some of their toys to give to needy children. Michelle spent one afternoon turning a shoe box into a tiny bed. Into this bed, she placed her favorite doll, covered with a quilt her grandmother had helped her make. This was the gift she asked her father to donate.

By 11, she had amassed an impressive collection of stuffed animals, many of them gifts from her grandmother. She was especially fond of a bassett hound she had named "Fido."

Fifteen-year old Michelle worked weekends in a nursing home, a job she held for over two years. She enjoyed chatting with the older people and then repeating some of their stories to her parents over dinner. Through a co-worker named Sue, she met her first boyfriend, Stuart, then 18. Because Michelle, like her mother, was rather insecure, having a boyfriend was very important to her.

As a 16-year-old, Michelle was still affectionate toward her parents, although she didn't share as much with them as she had when she was younger. Activities with her friends took up most of her free time, and she worried much more about fitting in with the group than about her class rank or a future career.

When she was 17, shortly after her high school graduation, she moved in with Stuart and his mother. She and Stuart described themselves as "pre-engaged." Her parents weren't pleased with her decision. Stuart came from a troubled family and drank too much. His brother Brad had been in and out of jail. But they consoled themselves with the fact that the relationship appeared stable and Michelle seemed happy.

Over that summer, Michelle and Stuart began to socialize with an unambitious and often rowdy group of kids. Michelle longed to be accepted by the new gang, and she would do almost anything to win its approval. She often confided in these new friends, even though her parents doubted their sincerity. Several times that summer, she revealed to the other teenagers that she had thought of killing herself. They didn't believe her.

On Sunday, March 10, 1985, the familiar crowd gathered for a party at Stuart's house. Among the partygoers was Sue, the mutual friend who had introduced Michelle and Stuart. As the night wore on, a rumor began to circulate that Stuart had cheated on Michelle with Sue. Furious and upset, Michelle left and drove to her parents' house.

Her parents heard her come home in the middle of the night, but were not overly concerned. Sometimes Michelle slept at home when she had to work early the next morning.

The next morning, Michelle's mother woke her daughter up. "Call me at work if you need anything," she said. "I'll be home at the regular time."

After Michelle got out of bed, she returned to Stuart's house. Once inside, she climbed into her boyfriend's bed and pulled the blanket over her head. Then she pointed Brad's 22-caliber rifle at her head and pulled the trigger.

When Michelle's mother returned home that evening, she saw that Michelle was gone, but she had not left a note. Her nightgown lay on the floor in a heap.

After dinner, Michelle's mother was alone in the house. Her father was attending a school board meeting, and 13-year old Jenny was at a neighbor's house making maple syrup. As she washed dishes, her mother listened to their radio scanner. Because Michelle's father was a volunteer firefighter, the radio was always left on. Suddenly, an emergency tone sounded. An anxious voice described a "possible 10-54S" at Stuart's address.

In a panic, Michelle's mother called the local police and asked if an officer would find her husband at the meeting and send him home. She called Stuart's house next and asked to speak with Michelle. The police officer who answered said, "Someone is looking for her." As soon as Michelle's father came home, he called a neighbor to watch Jenny and the anxious parents drove to Stuart's house.

When they arrived, the house was eerily aglow in the flashing lights of the police cruisers. Michelle's father hoped aloud that Stuart's brother had gotten into some trouble again. Then they noticed Michelle's car parked in the driveway. Her father sprang from the car and hurried toward a longtime friend who was a sheriff.

"Is it Michelle?" he demanded.

"Yes," his friend answered.

"Is she . . . dead?" Michelle's father asked.

"Yes."

Two weeks after the tragedy, Michelle's father, still dazed and overwhelmed with grief, was forcing himself to clean out Michelle's car. He was having trouble reconciling himself to the idea that his beloved daughter had taken her own life. Could it have been murder? Some of Stuart's friends were strange, even scary. He had not asked Stuart for details, and Stuart had not offered any.

For some reason, he decided to pull the seats out of the car. Under the passenger seat, he found his old target pistol, a single-shot 22-caliber pistol. The mechanism had been fired, but the shell had never gone off. He realized then that Michelle had committed suicide.

"She had tried to use my gun to kill herself," he said. "But for some reason, when she tried to shoot it, the gun jammed. I believe that God wouldn't let her kill herself with my gun. He knew that would have devastated me."

Over the next few months, Michelle's father confronted the reality of his daughter's death and began trying to understand it.

"She suffered from low self-esteem," he admitted. "And she acted very impulsively, easily influenced by what her friends said and did. At the time she killed herself, she was not very happy with her life. Her job was adequate, but not fulfilling, and perhaps there were more problems in her relationship with Stuart than we were aware of. She knew that she had made us unhappy by moving in with Stuart."

As with some young suicides, a tragic combination of personal qualities and life circumstances led Michelle to pull the trigger in a moment of anguish. And it is highly likely that depression played a critical role as well. Undiagnosed mental disorders such as depression may play a part in as many as 90 percent of all completed teen suicides. Because so many teens mask the signs and symptoms of their disease, it may be that parents and friends aren't aware of such a disorder until it is too late.

"I know she didn't think it through," said her father, "because she cared for her family too much. If she could have known how much we would suffer, she would not have done this. Like so many kids who commit suicide, she didn't think beyond the bang."

Michelle was buried in the spring of 1985. Fido was buried with her.

2

An Overview

Young people have a lot of questions about suicide. It is not a topic that is widely discussed, and most teens do not know anyone who has committed suicide. Most teens have *thought* about suicide, however, and many have attempted it, making it very important that their questions be answered honestly and completely.

What Is Suicide?

When a person commits suicide, he kills himself *intentionally*. But once someone has died, it may be hard to determine whether or not he *intended* to kill himself. A 17-year old boy is found dead in his crumpled car at the bottom of a steep embankment. He was alone in the car when it happened. Accident or suicide? A young woman embarks on a mountain hike one winter day. Her body is discovered weeks later at the foot of a sheer cliff. Accident or suicide? If there is no suicide note (and less than 25 percent of young people who complete suicide leave a note), the question may linger. In these cases, learning about the person's life-style, and character, and her behavior in the several days before the death by interviewing her relatives and friends may help to determine the person's intent.

Suicide Statistics for Teens

About 5,000 15- to 24-year olds complete suicide in the United States each year; 2,000 are under the age of 20. Since 1950, suicide rates for adolescents between 15 and 19 years old have quadrupled. Today, suicide is the second-leading cause of death for this age group in this country, after accidents.

These figures are based on information gathered by the federal government, which gets the data from coroners and medical examiners. But when medical examiners responded to a survey on all suicides, 58 percent agreed that the real suicide rate might be as much as twice as high as the official number. Some suicides are listed as accidents if there is no suicide note, to help the family avoid the stigma attached to suicide. Police officers sometimes call fatal, one-car crashes "autocides" when they believe that a teenager used the car as a weapon to kill himself. But of the 19,000 teens and young adults who die in auto accidents each year, very few are listed as suicides. Even some homicides probably represent kids who have a "death wish" and deliberately put themselves in dangerous situations.

How Kids Kill Themselves

Most use guns. Others overdose on pills, hang themselves, take in car exhaust, or jump off bridges or tall buildings. There are a number of factors that influence a teenager's choice. He will choose a method that is available (does he live near a bridge?), that is familiar (can he load a gun?), and that has some meaning (drugs may seem like a peaceful way to go). In general, when a teen uses a more lethal method (such as a gun, hanging, or jumping) he is showing that he is more serious about killing himself than someone who uses a less dangerous method such as a drug overdose or surface wrist slashes. With these last methods, death is not as immediate. The teen has time to change his mind or be rescued showing, perhaps, that he was more ambivalent about dying.

The Suicide Attempt

A suicide attempt does not result in death. It is called an incomplete suicide, failed suicide, or unsuccessful suicide. There are many different levels of incomplete suicide—from weak suicide gestures to true attempts.

The 14-year old who pops a half-dozen aspirins in her mouth in front of her family after an argument has made a suicide gesture. The young man who has suffered bouts of serious depression for years and finally tries to hang himself in the woods, only to be rescued unexpectedly, made an attempt. A suicide *gesture* is regarded as a cry for help that uses the "language" of self-destructive behavior. In a true suicide *attempt,* a teen intends to die and chooses a dangerous enough method to accomplish this, but he or she is saved by an unexpected rescue or an equipment failure, for instance.

Most suicide gestures and attempts involve girls who take drug overdoses. Even though such actions may not seem serious, anyone who displays self-destructive behavior is at risk for other more serious attempts, or for a completed suicide. In the same way that rehearsing for a play helps remove stage fright, some attempts help to reduce ambivalence about "the real thing."

How Many Teens Attempt Suicide?

You already know why it is hard to determine how many teens complete suicide each year. It is even harder to know how many teenagers *attempt* suicide each year, since about seven out of every eight attempts are not serious enough to require hospitalization and may go unreported. There may be as many as 500,000 attempts by young people every year. Experts have estimated that for high school students, there are 100 to 200 attempts for every actual suicide, while for college-age students, the ratio of attempts to completed suicides is about 10 to 1. It is estimated that every minute of every day in this country, a teen attempts suicide, and every $1\frac{1}{2}$ to 2 hours, a teen dies.

What do these statistics really mean? Glance around at the kids in your homeroom. In an average high school class of 30 students, two or three of them have attempted suicide.

Male and Female Differences

Girls are much more likely to attempt suicide and boys are much more likely to complete suicide. Experts know that males *commit* suicide five times more often than females, and they estimate females *attempt* suicide five to six times more often than males. This is true of all ages.

A related difference between the sexes is the tendency of boys to use more violent methods, such as guns, jumping, or hanging. It is because boys choose means that offer less chance of rescue that they complete suicide more often than girls. Of the 15- to 24-year olds who completed suicide in 1990, 57 percent were boys who died of gunshot wounds.

Suicidal girls usually opt for drug overdoses or wrist-slashing. Some have suggested that this is because girls want to avoid disfiguring their bodies.

Differences Among Minorities

Suicide rates have always been higher for white teens than black teens. The rate for African-American boys, however, has increased more dramatically than those of whites in the last thirty years. Being rejected, discriminated against, and pushed outside of society's mainstream causes low self-esteem and rage. In New York City, where many African Americans live in tenement buildings, over half of the reported suicides by African Americans are by jumping from rooftops.

Hispanics had previously ranked relatively low in suicides, attributed to the close, extended family network. But even rates for this group are increasing as the family loosens its reins on its teens and the language barrier presents difficulties in relationships outside of the immediate family.

Native Americans between 15 and 20 years of age are at a high risk for suicide. Their suicide rate is as much as 10 times the national average. Factors such as alcoholism, depression, unemployment, racism, lack of connection to spiritual heritage, and the prevalence of guns account for the variation in rate among different tribes. The Native-American adolescent is pulled between two cultures, and he may feel he belongs with neither.

Suicidal Thoughts

One study reported that 63 percent of high school students admitted having had thoughts about suicide at some point in their lives. This is due in part to the fact that young teens are just beginning to realize that they will not live forever. Some researchers have suggested that everyone at some time will mull over the idea of suicide. It is what the person does with those feelings that matters. Thoughts of suicide are not dangerous unless they become frequent or a teen threatens to act on them.

There is a generally accepted scale of potential danger. A suicidal thought is not as significant as a suicide wish and a wish is not as dangerous as a specific plan of action. A suicide plan may lead to an attempt. And about one in ten of those who attempt will ultimately complete. But if an individual's behavior seems to be moving up the scale toward suicide, there is a need to act.

Indirect Suicide or Chronic Self-Destructive Behavior

People who take dangerous risks are said to be exhibiting indirect self-destructive behavior. Some people hasten death through heavy smoking or drinking, or by ignoring a serious illness. Others mock death through "games." Death-oriented teenagers play "Chicken," in which two cars drive toward each other at a high speed. The driver who turns his car out of the path of the other is considered the chicken. Another extraordinarily dangerous game is Russian roulette, in which a person spins the cylinder of a revolver loaded with one bullet, aims the muzzle at his head, and pulls the trigger.

Some teens are aware that they have a death wish. They willingly gamble with death, leaving the actual decision up to "fate." Others don't regard their reckless behavior as an indication of their desire to commit suicide.

Cluster or Copycat Suicides

Cluster suicide and *copycat suicide* are the phrases used to describe several suicides that occur together or, more often, a series of suicides occurring one after the other. One individual's death by suicide leads other young people to commit copycat suicides. The concept of cluster suicides is not recent. In 1774, Johann Wolfgang von Goethe published a popular book called *The Sorrows of Young Werther* about a young man who commits suicide. The book was blamed for causing impressionable teenagers to take their own lives, and was banned. This is why the copycat syndrome is sometimes call the "Werther effect." In some cases, however, clusters are triggered by traumatic deaths in the community that were not suicides.

This is primarily an adolescent phenomenon, and it happens because teenagers are not only dramatic, but are very sensitive to actions by their peers. A suicide by another teenager has the same effect as a suicide by a family member. Suicide goes from being an idea to being an action.

In recent years, cluster suicides have received attention within the scientific community. According to the research, those most in danger of falling prey to the cluster syndrome are family members and friends of those who died, those who have previously attempted suicide, and those without a strong support system at home or in the community.

Although they account for no more than 1 to 5 percent of all youth suicides, cluster suicides are important to examine because in most cases they can be prevented. An example of a community with a good system in place to prevent cluster suicides is Bergenfield, New Jersey. After several teen suicides there in 1987, a Community Response Team was organized, made up of school teachers and counselors, ministers, town leaders, and mental health professionals. The team started a crisis hotline and opened a teen drop-in center with social workers. Recent high school dropouts were identified and visited by outreach workers to prevent them from feeling alone and suicidal.

Suicide Worldwide

Suicide is an international problem. As far as we know, suicide has existed in all types of societies throughout history. The economic, social, and political conditions within each country seem to influence the suicide rate. It makes sense that the seeds of suicide are planted in the culture. One culture in particular that has one of the world's highest youth suicide rates is Japan. Several factors contribute to these suicide statistics. The culture is more accepting of suicide than other cultures. For centuries, *hara-kiri,* or *seppuku,* in which a warrior disemboweled himself with his sword, was considered the honorable way to avoid dishonor. Soldiers often killed themselves rather than surrender to the enemy. And Japanese kamikaze pilots during World War II were trained to make suicidal crash attacks. Clearly, in specific instances, suicide has been a tradition in Japan. Thus the concept is a more familiar one to Japanese young people than to Spanish teens, for example.

In addition, there are not many people or organizations providing emotional support to young people in Japan. There is a conflict in their country between modern and traditional values, and young people often find themselves without anyone who understands what being a teen today means. Because Japanese children are discouraged from expressing hostile or negative thoughts, they tend to keep their feelings inside.

Competition among Japanese youth is fierce, and success is extremely important. To fail means to bring disgrace upon both oneself and one's family. The fear of failure or perceived failure is very damaging to a young person's sense of self-esteem. For Japanese teenagers, success is gauged by one criteria: acceptance into a respected university. Children are raised to prepare for the day of testing that will determine whether or not they will be eligible to attend a certain college. The system is referred to as "Examination Hell."

All of these factors combine to make the Japanese society one that fosters youth suicide. In Chapter 5, we will take a closer look at how society in general can influence an individual's suicidal tendencies.

The Stigma of Suicide

The shame felt by a suicide victim's family and by people who have attempted suicide stems from centuries of persecution. In Athens, Greece, long ago, the body of a suicide victim was buried outside the city and the hand that ended his life was cut off and buried elsewhere. Some ancient Greeks believed that when a person committed suicide, it meant that he was worthless.

During the Middle Ages, many European countries followed traditions that punished suicide victims and their families. In some cases, the body of a person who committed suicide would be burned, tossed into the dump, or dragged through the streets. In England as recently as the 17th century, a person who committed suicide was treated like a murderer, with his body buried at a crossroads with a stake piercing the heart.

In the years that followed, many governments, including our own, enacted laws making attempted suicide a crime. Suicide attempters were whipped or sent to prison. Most religions, as well, condemned suicide as a sin, saying that only God could take away life. In addition to these laws and traditions surrounding suicide, there was the widespread belief that suicidal people were insane.

There have been exceptions to this view of suicide as something shameful. Within the Eskimo culture, custom dictated that an old or sickly Eskimo would expose himself or herself to the elements (in other words, knowingly freeze to death), ensuring that the tribe would not have to support someone who was unproductive. But there has never been a society that approved of *youth* suicide.

While these ancient reactions to suicide do not take place on a large scale anymore, the shame and stigma remain.

Our society doesn't deal well with the issue of death and grieving in general. Suicide only complicates things.

Part II

Why?

"What could possibly be so bad in a 14-year old's life?" asked one mother who desperately searched for answers to her daughter's suicide.

Of all the questions posed about teen suicide, "Why?" is the one asked most often. Why would a 16-year old varsity basketball player from a close, middle-class family, shoot herself in the head? Why would a 19-year old college freshman with a B-average and a busy social life hang himself in his dorm room? WHY? WHY? WHY? We cannot ask the only ones who know for certain. They are no longer here. But we can assume that individual traits, family circumstances, and social forces combine to create a teenager who eventually comes to consider suicide the only available option.

We not only ask "Why this child?" but "Why so many more children now than 30 or 40 years ago?" The answer to this question lies in the social changes that have occurred so rapidly in the United States and the difficulty many of us are having adjusting to them.

3

The Suicidal Individual

For each teen who completes suicide, there are unique reasons. Each suicide is different; the events that bring a teen to the point of self-murder are different. But the anguish and despair that the young person feels just before pulling the trigger or jumping off the bridge are very much the same. The sense of being desperately trapped is universal. In every case, the young person sees suicide as the only means of escape, the only option left.

Most teenagers who attempt suicide are ambivalent, which means that they want to live as much as they want to die. A suicidal teen wants her intense emotional pain to end. She may see suicide as the only way to end that pain.

Typically, a suicidal adolescent has been troubled by a wide range of problems for a long period of time. There is a consistent, underlying unhappiness. Then, a trigger event, the final straw, makes death seem more appealing than life, and makes suicide seem like the answer. The last straw might be parents announcing a divorce, moving to a new town, getting pregnant, or failing a course. Such an event seems to take on inflated significance in the eyes of the adolescent. A failed course, for example, represents complete failure. The suicidal adolescent develops increasing tunnel vision, in which suicide eventually becomes the only possible response.

In general, teenagers do not have the perspective that adults have. Young people don't yet have the life experiences that teach them that things change and feelings change. Each day that passes without a phone call from a boyfriend, or without a nod of approval from the popular crowd, might as well be a year. Many young people don't understand that an intensely hurtful problem today will not seem that significant in another week or two. They do not understand that there are ways to solve problems and people who want to help.

One expert described a suicidal youth this way: He feels *hapless*, imagining that his life is cursed and that he's had more than his share of bad luck. He feels *hopeless* and cannot see how things could get better. He feels *helpless*, believing that no matter what he does to try to improve his life, it will make no difference. This is how I imagine Brian must have felt just before he committed suicide.

I spoke to Brian's parents five years after their 12-year old son shot himself. His mother told me that this was the year she expected to feel some of the burden of his death lifted from her. He would have graduated from high school this year, she told me, and in a different way he would have been leaving her behind when he went off to college.

Brian's Story

Brian's story begins in 1985, when his father left the Air Force to work as a geologist for a Dallas oil company. Brian, his older sister Brenda, and his mother stayed behind in Oklahoma for more than a year. The family decided that it was worth being separated to allow Brenda to finish high school and Brian to make the transition from elementary school to middle school.

During Brian's 1986 spring break, he and his mother went to Dallas to select the school he would attend when they moved. Brian chose a public school open to children district-wide that seemed to offer the structure that he liked. Although he worried that his grades (As and Bs) might not be good enough, the school did offer him admission for the next year.

Brenda, Brian, and their mother moved to Dallas in June of 1986. His parents had chosen the neighborhood carefully. With a pool and tennis courts, its own swim team and holiday parades, it felt like a small town within the big city.

His parents encouraged Brian to join the swim team, but he didn't want to. Brian had been involved in Boy Scouts when they lived in Oklahoma, so his parents got information on the scout troop in their new area. He wasn't interested. Because Brian was mechanically inclined and interested in trains and planes and how things worked, his father signed up for the Civil Air Patrol, which took them flying half a dozen times. Brian decided he didn't want to fly anymore. After that, his father joined an athletic club so that he and Brian could play raquetball together.

In September, Brenda left for college and Brian entered the seventh grade at his new school. Brian had a history of throwing up just before the first day of school every year. His queasy stomach acted up whenever he was upset or worried. It was the same this year, but he managed to make it through the first day. As in previous years, he started feeling better as he got used to the routine.

Because Brian was a shy boy, he found it difficult to make friends in his new school. He worried about failing and being asked to leave the school, even though he was on the honor roll after the first semester. The school's strict rules made him anxious. There was little time to move from one class to another, and teachers disciplined students who talked when they were not supposed to, or who were late for a class. Through a stroke of bad luck, Brian was unfairly singled out twice by teachers, once for tardiness and the other time for talking in class. In neither instance had he been at fault, and he took the reprimands very hard.

At home, his mother rarely punished Brian because he never needed it. A scolding, perhaps, but even that upset him. In elementary school, he'd had the same teacher for several years, and she was aware of his sensitivity and his desire to do everything perfectly. When she once asked him a question that he didn't know the answer to, his face went white. She decided not to call on him after that unless he had his hand up. None of his new middle-school teachers noticed that he was especially sensitive.

All during the fall, Brian missed his sister. His parents were preoccupied with Brenda as well. It was her first year away from home, and they felt that as a freshman in college on a basketball scholarship, she needed extra support. They called her frequently and talked about her over dinner.

The holiday season approached without the usual gatherings of relatives and friends. Because they were so new in town, Brian's family didn't know very many people. For the first time, Brian didn't get excited about the idea of Santa Claus. He asked his mother for laser tag. She discouraged him, reminding him that she didn't like toys that imitated guns. She was happy when, about a week before Christmas, he changed his mind and told her that he would like some computer games instead. But then he told her why: "I wouldn't have anyone to play tag with."

"I knew it was true," his mother said later, "but as an adult I also knew that it would blow over—he'd make new friends soon enough. But Brian wasn't thinking like an adult, he was thinking like a 12-year old." Every day that passed without a friend was like a year to the lonely and sensitive boy.

Brenda's arrival cheered Brian up. She had several weeks off for the holidays. The family returned to Oklahoma over Christmas to visit Brian's grandparents on their farm. Because Brenda had been away, she had lots of stories to share with the relatives. Brian played with his cousins, accompanying them for target practice near the pond. Brian's father, a Viet Nam veteran, had taught his son how to use a gun. One cousin later remembered that Brian had seemed overly interested in the gun he had used that day. It was his father's gun, which was kept in a zippered case under a bed at home, with the bullets stored in another room.

In the week between Christmas and New Year's Day, Brian complained of headaches. On New Year's Eve, the family was together at home. In past years, family friends would have joined them, but this year there was no party. The next day, the family went to watch the Cotton Bowl parade. Brian was restless. Within a day or two, Brenda returned to college.

On Saturday, January 3, Brian and his father played raquetball. Afterward, his father took him shopping to spend some of his Christmas money. His mother asked him about a book report that was due soon. He said, "Mom, I've got that taken care of." She thought it was strange that she hadn't even seen him reading the book.

School started again on Monday, January 5. At about 10 PM the night before, Brian's mother went in to ask him what time he wanted to get up. He was standing in his room, staring straight ahead. Although she thought it seemed odd, she kissed him good-night and went to bed herself. Suddenly, Brian was shaking her to wake her up. "I don't feel well, Mom," he said.

His mother got him some medicine to soothe his stomach and tucked him back into bed. She was used to the routine by now. She knew he would feel better after the first day of school was over, just as he always did. She found a book of fancy cars that he had received for Christmas. "Why don't you look through this," she suggested, thinking that it would take his mind off school. She went back to her own room. When she awoke later, she noticed that his lights were out.

The next morning, Brian's father left early for work. When Brenda telephoned, Brian talked to her for a while. He had missed her since her return to school. Brian was still complaining about a stomachache, but he didn't have a fever, and he wasn't throwing up.

His mother knew that she couldn't keep Brian home—he wasn't really sick and he had to have that "first day" eventually. But she decided to let him stay home for the morning and just attend the afternoon classes. Although Brian said that he was afraid he might throw up in school and be embarrassed, he finally agreed to go after lunch. His mother put quiet music on the stereo and covered him with a blanket. She periodically took his temperature and asked him how he was feeling.

At noon, Brian ate the peanut butter sandwich that his mother made for him. It was chilly, so she decided to warm up the car while he gathered his school books and coat. After she waited in the car for a few minutes, Brian came to the door. "I'll be out in a minute," he said. The look on his face said, "Don't hurry me." She waited for what seemed like a very long time and finally decided to see what was keeping him.

When she stepped into his room, he was lying on the floor. Blood was still running out of two holes in his head. His father's gun, the same gun he had used at Christmas time for target practice, lay beside him. He was still breathing, and moaning softly. His mother called an ambulance and held him while they waited for help, telling him how much she loved him.

Brian died on Tuesday, January 6, 1987, less than nine months from the day they moved to Dallas. For such a sensitive boy, those nine months without a close friend might as well have been 90 years. But was it worth dying over? Perhaps Brian did not understand the finality of death. He had never experienced death, not even the death of a pet.

"It should never have happened in our family," his mother told me. "There was no divorce, no drug or alcohol use, no abuse. But since it did, it could happen in any family."

What Puts Some Individuals at Risk

Certainly the social climate and family issues contribute to the suicide rate, but there are particular individuals who are "suicidal time bombs." They are at risk because of events that have happened in their lives, such as a significant loss, or because of certain biological or personal characteristics like depression or drug addiction.

Loss. "I had nothing left," Bill responded when asked why he had attempted to eletrocute himself.

The circumstances that trigger suicide almost always center around loss. Some losses are part of every teen's life, like the loss of carefree childhood. And all teens lose their parents as perfect, all-powerful heroes—suddenly their teenagers see their shortcomings.

Other losses are not universal but are common. If a teen loses his popular girlfriend, he may lose status with his peers. When an older brother or sister goes off to college, as Brenda did, the children left behind feel a loss.

Moving to a new area or state causes teens to feel the kinds of losses that are usually associated with death or divorce. A young person loses his house, his room, his school, his territory, and perhaps even his pets when his family relocates. Most important is the loss of friends and the trauma of trying to fit in with a new peer group. And teens often resent the sense that they had no say in the move, that their opinion was not sought. Many adolescents whose families move report feeling depressed. When that depression is not buffered by an ability to adapt, or by strong, sustaining supportive relationships, then it might precipitate suicide, as it did with Brian.

Some losses are not as typical, such as the death of a parent. "My real dad died when I was in the fourth grade," one teen told me. "He was an alcoholic, went into a coma, and never came out. I know I'm not very important to my stepfather." A youngster who has lost a parent to death feels abandoned, and angry at being left behind. Over 50 years ago, parental death was recognized by at least one researcher as common in the history of suicidal young people.

Divorce involves many losses, including the loss of a familiar family structure and the loss of one parent in the home. Divorce will be discussed in more detail in the chapter on suicide and the family, Chapter 4.

Drug and Alcohol Abuse. Sometimes when we ask "Why?" what we are asking is "Why this troubled kid and not that one?" Often, the difference between the teen who makes the fatal move and the one who stops herself in time is drugs or alcohol. Drugs and alcohol make a person less in control and less inhibited. And after the initial high, drugs cause depression.

The sense of caution and awareness of danger that may normally keep even a very depressed person from acting on a suicidal impulse disappears when drugs or alcohol are involved. Some estimate that half of all teens who commit suicide were using drugs or drinking just before their deaths. For those who attempt suicide, the number may be 75 percent.

In addition to eliminating a measure of caution and impairing thinking, drugs and alcohol are dangerous in and of themselves. An overdose or the wrong combination of drugs can kill. Certainly the more addicted a young person becomes, the greater the chance that the abuse will lead to serious injury or death.

Depression. Millions of Americans suffer from depression. Depression is a disease that produces physical, emotional, and mental symptoms. Without treatment, it can lead to suicide. One out of every seven severely depressed people will complete suicide in his or her lifetime. With treatment, 90 percent of depressed people recover.

Some people have one episode of depression, often triggered by a deep loss or rejection, while others have many episodes. Still others suffer so much that they can't function. The depressed teenager is often apathetic and withdrawn, preoccupied wtih self-destructive thoughts. He feels hopeless and takes no pleasure in ordinarily enjoyable activities. He makes no future plans. A history of loss, abuse, parental conflict, and suicide or alcoholism in the family are common.

Brian was typical of many depressed children, because he tended to internalize his fears rather than talk about them. His anxiety showed up in physical symptoms like chronic headaches, stomachaches, and disturbed sleeping patterns. He also stopped taking an interest in activities that used to excite him.

Doctors know that changes in brain chemistry sometimes cause depression and suicidal feelings; they also know that stress and unhappiness can lead to biochemical brain changes. It is hard to say which comes first: the chemical changes or depressed feelings. Most agree that the two are so connected that either one can come first, and then they reinforce each other.

Researchers believe that several dozen chemicals affect mood, although serotonin has received the most attention. We now have drugs that control depression by altering particular chemicals in the brain. Psychotherapy works well for people who are not severely depressed. Most often, a depressed person will use both.

Lack of coping skills. The suicidal teen has not learned from a stable adult role model how to solve, or even cope with, his problems. Some researchers believe that it is rejection or abuse in someone's early years that leads him to feel that he isn't competent to solve problems on his own. He may try to escape by using alcohol or drugs, skipping school, stealing, running away from home, having sex with anyone, or fighting. Sadly, these ways of "handling" problems only lead to more—and worse—problems.

For those teens who feel unable to cope with their lives, feelings of helplessness and hopelessness soon emerge. They stop believing that things will get better. They feel that nothing will improve their situations and that the only option left is suicide.

Anxiety. A University of Michigan study of teenagers found that a tendency to worry is an important factor in determinining who may be suicidal. Teenagers tend to worry most about grades and tests in school. A different group of researchers said that one-quarter of college freshmen will consider attempting suicide, due in large part to the new academic pressures.

Some Other Reasons Teens Commit Suicide

Some teenagers reveal through suicide notes or interviews after their attempts specific reasons for wanting to take their own lives.

An overreaction. More than 80 percent of nonfatal suicides are impulsive reactions to brief crises. A girl who learns that her boyfriend has been unfaithful may slash her wrists, for example. There's more to it, though. Not everyone who loses a boyfriend commits suicide or wants to. But for some, the feeling of rejection that comes with a breakup is a "last straw" event. Perhaps even unbeknownst to the teen, suicidal feelings had been building. There has been a history of low self-esteem or a series of losses. Suddenly, one traumatic event seems to represent to the teen all of the bad things that have come before. It brings back all past losses and feelings of failure and makes the current problem seem huge.

Revenge. "My father will be sorry when I'm dead," thinks the 16-year-old daughter contemplating suicide. Maybe he will, but she won't be around to see it. Some young people don't understand that death is final. No one returns from death to witness the reactions of those whose lives will be turned upside down by a suicide. Despite this fact, some teens do feel so rejected or betrayed by those whom they feel should love them that they decide that suicide is the only way to really get even.

Control. Perhaps because teenagers are required to follow so many rules at home and in school, some become obsessed with controlling every aspect of their lives, including its ending. By killing herself, a girl feels that she has "controlled" her death, determining when, where, and how she will die.

Romeo and Juliet. Romeo and Juliet, two "star-crossed" teenage lovers separated by a family feud, end up by killing themselves. Love and death are often connected in books and plays. Often, lovers plan to be reunited in death. Teenagers, romantic by nature, may feel that completing suicide is one way to join someone who has died. This is why some suicide experts have said that the "reunion" theme so common in funerals or memorial services should be downplayed when the victim is a teenager. Some classmates may misinterpret the message and seriously consider suicide.

The Romeo and Juliet theme is also related to completed suicides or attempts in which a teenager decides to "die for love." In most of these cases, girls make rather weak attempts to try to win back a boyfriend. Research conducted at colleges revealed that problems with romantic relationships were one of the most frequent causes of suicide attempts.

Attention. A teenager may feel that she will attract more attention by dying than by living. Suicide is her ticket to fame. She imagines being a glamorous or romantic figure in death. She fantasizes about people crying at her funeral. What she has overlooked is the fact that she won't be able to witness the funeral, or to enjoy the attention. She will be dead.

School officials are becoming more aware of the dangers of a lavish memorial service for a student who has died from whatever cause. A great deal of attention focused on a dead classmate might encourage others who want similar recognition.

Starting over. One 13-year old boy wrote in a suicide note to his parents, "I'm going to a new life . . . I always wanted a second chance." Teens who kill themselves in an attempt at rebirth or immortality are usually suffering from severe mental problems or have spiritual belief systems that include reincarnation.

4

Suicide and the Family

Parents—or stepparents—are not the cause of a child's suicide. Nor are brothers and sisters, aunts, uncles, and grandparents. No one can make another person kill himself or herself. But there are certain things that happen within families that can push a young person to attempt suicide. In fact, many have attributed the rising teen suicide rate to the fact that the American family seems to be falling apart. When you read Jennifer's story, as told to me by her father, brother, and grandmother, you will understand how family circumstances can have a deadly impact on a young person's self-esteem and desire to live.

Jennifer's Story

Because Jennifer was only three years old when her mother died, nobody told her that it was a suicide. In a last letter to her husband, Jennifer's mother wrote that she loved him and asked that his mother take care of their two children until he could remarry. She wanted him to find a woman who would be a kind and loving stepmother. After her death, Jennifer's father took Jennifer and her brother, Dan, to live with his parents. Both children soon became very attached to their grandparents.

Shocked by the loss and anxious to put his family back together, Jennifer's father remarried within a year. Betty, his new wife, moved in with her three daughters from a previous marriage. As the youngest, and most timid, of the five children, Jennifer was lost in the confusion. Betty, jealous of the strong bond between Jennifer and her father, tried to create problems between them. She also discouraged Jennifer and Dan from seeing their grandparents.

Jennifer's father then realized that his marriage to Betty had been a mistake. They divorced after four years. Still desperate to provide the loving stepmother that his first wife had wanted for her children, Jennifer's father married Leslie within a year of his divorce from Betty. Jennifer was now 9 years old.

Leslie, an oppressive and domineering woman, was as threatened by the close relationship between Jennifer and her father as Betty had been. She, too, tried to limit the time that the two of them spent together, although her husband's job as a race track veterinarian meant that he was already gone for months at a time. Jennifer missed him desperately when he was working. In one letter to him she announced, "You will be home in 20 days! I am counting the days as I mark them off on my calendar." To accommodate his job, the family moved frequently as well.

Jennifer suffered quietly under Leslie's belligerent mothering for several years. At 10, she loved softball and was an avid Snoopy fan. In her journal, she wrote that she wanted a "flying Snoopy who can go anywhere, even to Heaven." Her brother, Dan, described her as a gentle child who was sensitive to other people's feelings, and was herself hurt very easily. Jennifer's grandmother said, "If Jennifer put a little pan on a big burner, Leslie would scold Jennifer until the little girl shook with fear."

It wasn't until she was 15 that Jennifer learned the shocking details of her mother's death. Not long after, Jennifer swallowed a handful of aspirin across the street from the house where her mother spent her final days. When Jennifer was recovering in the hospital after her attempt, Leslie attacked her for trying to get attention. In uncharacteristic defiance, Jennifer decided to call her stepmother "Leslie" instead of "Mom." Despite Leslie's loud protests, Jennifer never wavered.

Over the next year, Jennifer made between 20 and 30 suicide attempts, most of them overdoses. She seemed unable to cope with her problems, especially with Leslie, whom she regarded as her biggest problem. She would react calmly to Leslie's repeated attacks but then would disappear and swallow a bottle of pills. Once she drove off in her grandmother's car and was missing for over eight hours. Her father finally spotted the car parked across the street from the hospital. Jennifer was sleeping off an overdose in the back seat.

After one trip to the hospital, the doctors sent Jennifer to her grandmother's house to recuperate, with orders that Leslie was not to visit. Leslie immediately showed up, insisting that she was not the cause of the attempts. Jennifer drifted in and out of several hospitals, even saving up her medication there and attempting to overdose.

One New Year's Day, as she was watching the parade on television with her father and brother, she suddenly got up and went upstairs to her room. Within minutes, her father and brother watched in horror as her body hurled past the window of the room in which they were sitting. She broke several bones and was hospitalized for a month. Her father, grandmother, and Dan took turns staying with her, since the hospital required constant supervision due to her suicidal tendencies.

The year that followed was relatively trouble free, with Jennifer spending an extended period in Florida alone with her father. She enjoyed school there and got good grades, as she always had. After that visit, she wrote to her father, "We had such a good time together . . . I am sure that we will be able to stay this close forever." She also wrote other letters, begging to accompany her father if he had to go on another long trip. Back home, Leslie still made things difficult for Jennifer, and in more than one letter to her father she wrote, "Please don't leave me with Leslie anymore."

"Leslie still fights with Dad and calls him bad names," she wrote in a letter to her brother. "I worry about Dad . . . I feel so sad that he has not had a better life . . . I feel guilty when I'm happy knowing that Dad has been treated the way he has been." "Maybe," she wrote in another letter to her grandparents, "it would help if I was not here. . . . It seems I just add to Leslie's anger."

When the family moved to Ohio during Jennifer's junior year in high school, she became very active in her church, an interest that Leslie mocked. As she was driving home from a church youth group meeting one evening, Jennifer was involved in a serious car accident. She spent the next year recovering from injuries to her pelvis and legs, undergoing seven operations and hours of painful physical therapy.

With Leslie making life increasingly difficult for her, Jennifer decided to move in with the family of her church's youth pastor, barely speaking to her own family for the next year. To keep her distance from Leslie, she decided that she had to distance herself from her father and brother as well. She returned to high school to graduate with her class, still suffering from physical pain as a result of the accident.

By that summer, she began showing more interest in her family again. She went to lunch with Dan. She called her father. In the fall, she went to a Christian college with several other members of her church youth group. Three weeks into the semester, though, she called her father, asking him to pick her up. She was not happy. She returned with him to New Hampshire, where he had recently moved with Leslie and Nathan, their young son. Jennifer found a job as a waitress and talked of going to college in the area, perhaps to pursue nursing.

But soon she admitted to her father that she was having "bad thoughts" again, thoughts of suicide. Cut off from her therapist and her group of church friends, she was beginning to feel depressed. Her father quickly found her a new therapist. She went for her first visit on a Wednesday. She liked the therapist and thought that she would make progress with him. He told her that he wouldn't be able to see her for two weeks.

On Sunday, Jennifer's father found an unfinished letter in her desk drawer. It read like the beginning of a suicide note, but he couldn't be sure. And he didn't know how to ask her about it, since he thought she might become upset knowing that he had looked in her room. He decided to keep a careful eye on her.

One week later, six weeks after he had picked Jennifer up from college, her father took the whole family to brunch. Jennifer seemed very content, happy even. He noticed that she even drank a glass of champagne, something he had never seen her do.

That evening, he waited for Jennifer to return from her waitressing job. When she failed to come home on time, he drove to the restaurant. It was locked up. Some employees in the parking lot told him that Jennifer had not been to work at all that day. All through that night and into the next day he waited by the phone, knowing from experience that driving around looking for her was usually fruitless.

The phone rang after lunch. It was a police officer calling from a motel in Marlborough, Massachusetts, 50 miles away. "I'm calling about your daughter," he said.

"Is Jennifer all right?" her father asked anxiously. He had asked that question so many times in the past five years. But this time, the answer was different.

"No," the police officer told him. "She's dead."

She was 19 years old.

Families at Risk

While some families that suffer a suicide are close and loving, many others are not. Many families with members at risk for suicide show certain, or similar, characteristics. There is usually a lack of communication, a poor relationship between the parents, long-term patterns of alcoholism or drug abuse, high parental expectations, and a family history of depression and suicide.

Adolescents need their families for financial and emotional support, but often they get neither. This leaves them feeling trapped and helpless. In some cases, parents are so troubled themselves that they cannot provide the stability and security that a teenager needs. They are not up to taking part in the push-pull relationship that enables a teenager to move from childhood to adulthood. Teens must be able to experiment with independence while continuing to take comfort in the safety of home and family. In even the best family situation, earlier problems between the parents and child are intensified during the teen years, often making the relationship uneasy.

Teens Talk about Their Families

I asked a number of high school juniors and seniors to tell me about their families. What follows is a sampling of their reactions to a number of family issues, and comments on why these issues affect a teenager's risk for suicide.

Mattering.

. . . I know I'm not very important in my Dad's family. They have two little kids—and I love the kids—but they're obviously more important to my Dad and stepmother than I am.

. . . My mother died when I was eight. My father acts indifferent or condescending toward me. He just bought an $8,000 boat, but he claims he can't afford $2,000 a year for my college tuition.

. . . I feel like an outsider in my own house. No one ever takes my feelings into account. When I have an opinion on any subject, I'm always put down.

. . . I don't see my dad very often. He never calls, not even on Christmas or my birthday. And when I ask him to do something with me, he's always too busy. It makes me feel very unwanted.

A teen needs to feel valued by her family. She needs to feel that she matters to her parents, that she is important to them. A teenager can have all of her material needs met but still feel unwanted.

An adolescent's feelings of self-worth are determined by how she thinks other people feel about her. Studies have shown a clear relationship between a teenager's self-esteem and his feeling that his parents care about him. Low self-esteem is a common characteristic of suicidal people of all ages.

Physical, emotional, and sexual abuse.

. . . My relationship with my father is very unstable. We have gotten into many fist fights. We even fought when I was in bed with a cast on my leg.

. . . My stepfather needs to have everything his way. He wants to have complete control over everything. One time, I ran down the stairs noisily and he made me walk up and down the stairs until he was satisfied with the way I did it. Yesterday he shoved a skinny 13-year-old because he had wandered onto our driveway.

. . . Last year my stepfather beat me up. I tried to run away and he came to the bus station while the bus was there. He beat me up again. This time the cops saw and I ended up in a foster home for two months. I was there through Christmas, which was horrible. Finally I moved in with my best friend and her family.

A lack of attention can be hurtful, but the wrong kind of attention from a parent can be devastating. Young people who have been abused are more likely to be suicide victims. The abuse can cause a teen to feel so much pain that death seems to be the only escape. After all, an abused teenager who hurts himself is simply imitating the way his parents have been treating him for most of his life.

Alcoholism or drug abuse.

. . . My dad was an alcoholic and went to AA. My mom said that lately he's been back to it, and it's really stressful. I feel like I can't trust him now.

. . . My father is a drug addict. When I was 10 years old, he had a cocaine party one Friday night. He taught me how to cut it with vitamins and how to draw lines. Then while the people were snorting, I stood by the table and held the money while they took turns. He had promised me the best Christmas ever but it never happened. The weird thing is that I love him with all my heart and I forgive him.

A family history of alcoholism can lead teenagers to engage in similar self-destructive behavior. A parent who abuses alcohol has a more difficult time being attentive to his or her child. And alcoholism is clearly linked to suicide. Children living with addicted family members are at a 30 percent higher risk for suicidal behaviors.

History of depression in the family.

. . . My mother is depressed a lot from a terrible childhood. I try to do all I can to help and make her happy. Sometimes it's stressful, but I understand and love her.

. . . My father is on medication for depression. It runs in his family. It makes me wonder if I will have some problems with depression, if I am predisposed to serious depression-related illnesses.

. . . My mom was sexually abused when she was young, and she is now in counseling for depression. I try to be supportive.

A suicidal teen may reflect his family's troubles. In one study of the families of teenagers who had killed themselves, nearly all of the teens' parents were depressed and had thought about suicide. And depression may be passed down from parents to children. Researchers have determined that children with a depressed parent stand a 20 to 30 percent chance of also being depressed.

Unrealistic expectations.

. . . I feel like I always let my parents down.

. . . I'm the oldest child and I've never met my parents' expectations of me. Now that I'm leaving home, I'm afraid my parents won't miss me, or will remember me as a failure. My sister seems to be doing so much better that I guess I'm afraid that she'll cover my tracks.

. . . My parents feel my grades are the only important thing in my life. I try my best, but that isn't good enough for them.

. . . I play hockey. Whenever I have a good game my parents don't acknowledge it. One time we were giving a friend a ride home after a win. My dad praised the friend for his two goals but never said anything to me.

Some parents unknowingly transmit the message: "I won't love you *unless . . .*" The "unless" might involve grades, sports achievements, or popularity. Often, these parents push their children to achieve what they weren't able to. Insecure parents see their children as status symbols rather than people, and feel that the number of trophies and awards the kids accumulate show how successful they are as parents.

A child's sense of self-worth may be so tied to top grades or outstanding athletic performances that a bad mark or an off game may be enough to make him think of suicide. Parents who have unrealistic expectations for their children are setting them up for failure.

Teens need to feel that they can set their own goals. Parents also need to reinforce their unconditional love for their children, love that is unrelated to any achievements.

The fairy-tale family.

. . . To outsiders our family appears perfect. My father never talks about problems. He ignores them, hoping they'll blow over.

. . . My parents discuss world problems, the news. They don't discuss problems about me, like sex or suicide. It's like they're scared that if they say it, it will happen.

Some families project a perfect image. There are no problems, or so it seems. Teens who are raised to believe that people should be constantly happy and have no troubles will be confused and depressed adults. No one's life is completely happy and trouble-free. The happiest people aren't the ones with the fewest problems, they are the ones with the best problem-solving skills.

Parents must teach their children how to deal with pain and problems, not how to ignore or avoid them.

Pain and problems are part of living. It is from stress that kids learn to cope. Teens who can cope are less likely to succumb to suicide.

Divorce.

. . . My parents separated when I was 11 years old. I had to choose between them when I was only 12. I didn't want to because I loved them both very much. I think that's why my Dad and I don't get along—because I chose my mother.

. . . I feel a lot of stress because I always have to defend my father.

. . . My parents divorced when I was a baby. I don't think I really know what a family is.

. . . My mom and dad divorced when I was two, and even though my dad lives five minutes down the road, he always makes up an excuse not to see me, or he doesn't show up when he's supposed to.

. . . My parents are divorced, but what has created most of the stress were the remarriages of both of my parents.

. . . My dad despises my mom for leaving him but he can't get to her anymore so he goes through me.

Rates of divorce and suicide climbed together during the 1960s and 1970s. Today, the United States has the world's highest divorce rate. Researchers have discovered that many young suicide victims come from families split by divorce. Divorce, like death, brings on feelings of anger, abandonment, guilt, sadness, and loss. In fact, divorce may be *harder* for youngsters to come to terms with than a parent's death.

One reason is that divorce is usually preceded by a lot of hostility and tension. And it is not as final as death. Children are often shuttled between parents, used as pawns by bitter adults. There also may be stepparents involved. Divorce brings less parental attention, less money, and less of a "home" atmosphere. Children can feel they are a large economic burden on the parent they live with and feel abandoned by the other parent. They also may feel partly responsible for the divorce. The older the child is when the parents divorce, the more difficult it is to accept.

Divorce does not have to be as stressful on children as it often is, however. Recently, researchers have begun to realize that it may not be the divorce that is the suicide risk factor, but the relationships the child has with both parents before and after. If divorced parents work to maintain strong ties with their children, divorce is much less stressful on them.

Family scapegoat.

. . . When I moved in with my Dad, everything was my fault. My brother could do no wrong. It was the worst time of my life—lots of yelling, hitting, stuff like that.

. . . Even when someone else does something wrong, my parents say it was learned from me, encouraged by me, or somehow done by me.

58

. . . It isn't so much that my parents blame me for everything, but they dwell on the wrong things that I do. They never comment on anything good that I've done.

Families plagued by hard times may choose one member to be the scapegoat. Everyone targets the scapegoat, blaming him for the bad things that have happened to the family. Maybe it is the weakest member of the family who is chosen, maybe the most rebellious. But constant anger and blame focused on that person will, over time, make him feel angry at himself and worthless.

Lack of communication.

. . . Sure we communicate. They tell me what to do, and I'm supposed to listen.

. . . My parents don't know how to talk. They only know how to scream and yell or give me the silent treatment.

One study of suicidal teens revealed that a major cause of their unhappiness was the feeling that their parents did not understand them. They did not feel able to express their concerns to their parents.

Parents must try to understand stress from an adolescent's point of view. To an adult, doing poorly on a test, not making the soccer team, or seeing your girlfriend holding hands with another guy do not seem particularly stressful. But from a teenager's perspective, these things can be devastating. Parents need to listen to what their children tell them, and validate their children's feelings.

5

Suicide and Society

About 100 years ago, a man named Emile Durkheim wrote about suicide. He believed that suicides were a result of how much control society had over an individual. Japanese kamikaze pilots during World War II are examples of people who were too controlled by their society. A homeless person without friends or family who hangs himself in an empty warehouse is an example of someone who does not feel *any* connection with society.

Suicide and society show a connection in other ways as well. Suicide rates can sometimes be related to world events. Rates drop during wartime, for example. During wartime do we as individuals feel a sense of unity and purpose? Or do we have a common enemy, a scapegoat for our anger and hostility? On the other hand, suicide rates rise during economic hard times and during times of national turmoil.

When researchers examine the dramatic rise in teen suicide during the past 30 to 40 years, they also look at the changes that have taken place in our society during that same period. Many have concluded that too many things changed too fast over a relatively short period of time, creating turmoil and upheaval. Everything from family structure to the weapons we manufacture have undergone dramatic change.

At least one researcher has noted that the rise in the suicide rate seems to correspond to an increase in the percentage of young people in the population. That is, as the baby boom generation approached adulthood, they brought a higher suicide rate with them. Perhaps this is because more peers means more competition for special recognition in school, jobs, and college slots.

By looking at the differences between life today and 40 years ago, we can begin to understand why the teen suicide rate has risen so rapidly.

Effect of Changes in Family Life

I spoke with Eleanor, who was a teenager in the 1940s and '50s, and with Anne, who is a teenager today, about their lives. (Anne slipped me a note when I spoke to her psychology class on teen suicide. Because she had thought of killing herself, she offered to be interviewed for this book.)

To be sure, not all teenagers today live like Anne, and not all teenagers of 45 years ago lived like Eleanor. But each story adds something to our understanding of how society has changed over the past two generations.

Eleanor's Story

I grew up in Chicago 40 years ago. There was a strong sense of neighborhood where I lived. All of my friends were from my neighborhood, and folks rarely moved in or out. We all lived within a few blocks of the neighborhood school and we walked there every day.

In our family, as in most, my father was the head of the house and my mother was the heart. He worked to support us, while she stayed home to take care of us. My parents had met as children, and they were married for nearly 50 years until my mother's death. Divorce was so uncommon that it never occurred to my brother and sister and me that families weren't permanent units.

Extended family played a very important role when I was a child. There were always relatives around to talk with and play with. Often there were multiple generations under one roof. For five years while my Uncle Art was in the service, my Aunt Pearl lived with us and helped my mother with the children and the house.

Many of our relatives lived close by, and they seemed to have a lot of time to spend with children. Back then, everyone retired by 65 and often didn't have the financial resources to travel or own winter homes in other parts of the country. They spent their free time involved in family activities, usually centered around grandchildren and neices and nephews. Birthdays and holidays were festive occasions, always celebrated with lots of relatives.

While we received a great deal of support from the family, there were a lot of expectations as well. It was important to behave and measure up. If you disgraced yourself, you disgraced your family. So along with the sense of belonging to a strong family unit came a sense of duty to make your parents proud of you. This, as well as the limited freedom kids had (most didn't have cars) and the constant supervision by relatives, kept us in line. I think it was easier then to do the "right thing" because there was not a lot of opportunity to do the wrong thing. Kids weren't often put in the position of being tempted. Drugs were unknown, and even smoking and drinking were not that common.

There was much more family control over the dating situation than there is today. On weekend evenings, I dated boys from my neighborhood or my church. My parents nearly always knew the boy's parents. It was very unusual that I would bring home a boy whom they had not already met. I would never have dated a Catholic boy, for instance, not being Catholic myself. Boys always called girls, always made the plans, always paid. We went to square dances, the movies, roller skating, or on hay rides. There were no sexual pressures. First of all, there was very little privacy. Often, my parents or my older brother drove me and my date to the movies and then picked us up. Also, the girls who were "easy" were not regarded as desirable dates.

My friends and I never went out during the week—those evenings were reserved for family time. The evening meal was always an important event. My mother took much of the afternoon to carefully prepare it and it was the time when we all sat down together to share our day's events. There was no such thing as "fast food." After dinner, we all helped to clean up (no automatic dishwashers!) and then we listened to the radio or, more often, we played board games. Monopoly was the family favorite, with checkers a close second. On summer evenings we played badminton or croquet. Often we'd go for a family drive after dinner. That was a big deal since we only had one car, and my father took it to work every day. We might drive to the park, or to get ice cream cones.

Everyone we knew belonged to a church. My mother was very active in church organizations, and we grew up belonging to church youth groups. We never missed the Sunday service. After church, we went to my grandparents' house. All of my cousins were there, my aunts, my uncles—all the relatives. Everyone lived close enough to get together at least once a week.

There were not a lot of choices in those days. Teenagers had realistic, sensible goals and expectations about what the future held. My older brother followed in my father's footsteps, acquiring a job in the same insurance company after graduating from college. My sister and I followed in my mother's footsteps, getting married and becoming full-time mothers and housewives. This sense of tradition was not always good, since girls who desired to be engineers or architects were discouraged from pursuing these goals. But there were fewer choices and thus less confusion. Life was ordered, traditional, and calm.

Anne's Story

I am sixteen years old. My parents divorced when I was nine. My Dad moved out. I didn't really understand what was happening, and my parents told me not to tell anyone about the divorce. One of my friends told me she saw my father, who was a teacher, kissing another woman in the teacher's room. He told me it wasn't true, but as it

65

turned out he was living with this other teacher after he left us. He gave us a different address, though.

The divorce was hardest on my older sister. She had lots of trouble accepting what was happening and was very hard to get along with. She started rebelling and sleeping around. We got into some fistfights. She moved out at 18 and recently had a baby. My Dad practically disowned her when she got pregnant, although now he sees the baby. She's not married but she's living with someone. He's not the father of the baby though, and he doesn't seem to treat her very well.

When my mother got remarried, I was very upset. I didn't like my stepfather at all. I remember sitting in my room and screaming, "Get out of my house!" But things have gotten better since. My father has remarried too, but I don't like my stepmother. She seems jealous of anyone who tries to get close to my father. I visit my father every other weekend, but I just sleep there. During the day I go out with my friends. Most kids go to parties and drink, or do drugs. I don't do that. Usually my friends and I just drive around and talk. I also like to go bowling. My Dad often cancels my visits, though, to go to Rhode Island to see his wife's family.

My Mom and I get along well. If I'm down, she'll ask me what's wrong. But it's hard to talk to her about a lot of things. I mean, she still thinks I'm a virgin. I don't sleep around or anything. Not with AIDS and STDs. But I've had boyfriends. I got a tatoo recently and I finally got up enough nerve to tell her. She said that she was disappointed in me, but that she's trying to understand.

My father's parents live in town, but since the divorce my grandmother hasn't been that nice to me. My father gets mad at me for not calling her on the phone, but when I do she acts very distant. The rest of his relatives live in another state. My mother's family lives about 50 miles away so we see them sometimes on holidays.

We've never belonged to a church. My father didn't have any use for religion, and after he left, I guess my mother thought it was too late for us to start going to Sunday School. I've only been to church a few times.

We don't really do much as a family. Sometimes we go camping, but most of my activities are with friends. I go out almost every night with my friends. I usually eat dinner with my mom and stepfather, but when my boyfriend is in town, I don't. I spend all of my evenings with him.

Both of my parents work. I need to get a job myself to pay for my car insurance and to pay for photography school. I'll have to work for a year after I graduate from high school to pay for 10 months at the school.

I have thought about suicide before. I've even thought about how I might do it. I feel trapped and unhappy about my boyfriend situation. My ex-boyfriend, who wants me back, abused me in some ways, and made me feel worthless. But he's changing. And we made a lot of plans together, like when we would get married. He even gave me two diamonds.

But now there's another guy that I am attracted to. He treats me better than my ex-boyfriend. But I still feel this attraction to my ex. Now they want me to choose. No matter who I choose, I won't be allowed to talk to the other one. I'll have to hurt someone. Sometimes I feel like I was put on this earth to hurt people. Life is very confusing.

Effect of Changes in Technology

With every new invention, life changes to accommodate it. Over the last four decades, the result often has been greater personal isolation, which is connected to teen suicide. Families don't chat or play board games after dinner anymore, they watch television. Superhighways take people away from each other easier and faster. Computers, whether for work or play, are solitary units. Perhaps the best example of an invention that has increased isolation is the popular Sony Walkman, a portable cassette player with headphones that only allows one person to listen at a time.

Improvements in technology nearly always involve speeding things up. Dinner can be ready in 10 minutes with a microwave oven. Numbers can be multiplied in seconds with a calculator. And yet human problems still take lots of time to solve. Pain still does not disappear rapidly. There are no quick fixes for hurt.

Pressures on Today's Teens

Young people are very concerned about being "normal." Sexual identities, for example, can cause a great deal of confusion. Some young men become so concerned by homosexual feelings that they attempt suicide. Several studies have shown that homosexual men and women attempt suicide up to seven times more often than heterosexuals.

Peer pressure is a phrase often used to describe the significance of teens to each other. As young people move beyond the family to forge new relationships, they are forging new identities. Children are defined by their parents; teens seek to be defined by their peer group. Friends help determine what a teenager thinks he is worth. If a teenager is not accepted by peers and becomes alienated from them, his feelings of self-worth drop significantly.

Teens are not only concerned with their friends, their studies, and their families. They are also concerned with world conditions: AIDS; global warming; recessions; nuclear war. In our parents' day, people believed that the future of the world was in God's hands. Now, it seems as if any power-hungry leader who gains control of the right buttons can end it for all of us. Teenagers need to anticipate a stable, secure future to avoid feeling hopeless and depressed. Some teens say that they may as well live for today, since no one is promising them a tomorrow.

Cars and guns are not new, but they are more accessible to teenagers than ever before, and such easy access adds to the national suicide crisis. Each year, about 19,000 teens and young adults die in car accidents in this country; some are surely suicides. Guns now account for the cause of death in almost two out of every three adolescent suicides in this country.

Drugs are a more recent health issue. And the drug problem in this country has become epidemic. As we have already seen, drug and alcohol abuse is involved in at least half of all suicides.

Suicide and the Media

Another way in which changes in society are said to have contributed to an increase in suicide concerns the media. Many who study youth suicide criticize newspapers, television, and films for how they treat the topic of suicide. For instance, the language used in describing completed suicides and attempted suicides is potentially dangerous to young listeners or readers. Often, teens who do not complete suicide "failed" and those who did complete it were "successful."

Television also increases our sense of helplessness. Our TV sets bring the horrors of war, crime, and famine into our living rooms, and yet we feel that there's nothing we can do to help. We feel too insignificant to make any difference. A feeling of helplessness is a leading characteristic of suicidal teens.

News reports. Some people feel that suicide becomes a more viable option to certain teens when they hear a news story of a completed suicide. We live in a country that thrives on freedom of the press, however. Can we stifle such reports? Should we? No. It has been proven that talking about suicide does not make anyone commit suicide. But the "talking" has to be done in a sensitive and conscientious way.

News reports should stress the tragedy of a suicide, not the sensationalistic details. Suicides should not appear glamorous or heroic. The victims should not seem to get more attention in death than they did in life. They should not become role models for other troubled teens.

Actually, the media can help *prevent* suicide. After reporting a case of suicide, for instance, a TV newscaster could list the telephone numbers of crisis hotlines or the names of counseling centers. Limited research suggests that when television shows give people direction after drawing them into the concept of suicide, potential suicides can be avoided.

Make-believe death and real death. Young people, especially, seem to favor movies and television shows that contain a lot of violence. Today's teenagers have witnessed about 15,000 television murders over their lifetimes. This desensitizes them; that is, they become numb to the violence. When viewers become used to a certain level of violence, television producers increase the violence to make us react. But this isn't "real" death: This is death in television land. Actors die on one show and reappear on another; they survive car crashes and comas, defying the odds over and over again. TV death doesn't seem final. Rather it seems quick, painless, and often glamorous.

At the same time that we are exposed to these fantasy deaths, we are less exposed to real death in our own lives. Death is not as commonplace as it was a century ago. It is rare for an infant or young child to die. Grandparents die in hospitals now, not in the home, surrounded by family members.

The constant exposure to "pretend" death and lack of exposure to real death makes it easier for a teen to pull a trigger or swallow a bottle of pills without fully understanding the consequences.

Television's instant solutions and perfect faces. Half-hour situation comedies and hour-long dramatic television shows have also been blamed for pushing teens toward suicide, although more indirectly. In most cases, these shows set up problems that are neatly solved within the program time allotted. The actors look perfect, say the right things, and come up with neat, quick solutions to often serious problems.

To a troubled teen who may have spent years *not* coming up with the answers, these shows reinforce his inability to cope. They do not accurately portray what problem-solving is all about. In real life, problems take a long time to work through. And no one looks perfect doing it.

Those television shows that directly address suicide can be beneficial by showing alternatives to suicide. Documentaries on depression or suicide can provide answers to desperate viewers. Informative, factual shows will help prevent suicide, while sensationalizing the tragedy without providing an educational component merely adds to the problem.

Part III

Prevention

Why should we try to prevent suicide? Doesn't anyone who wants to kill himself have the right to do so? We must try because we now know that people are suicidal for just a short time—the suicidal crisis is temporary. Once they are helped through the crisis, the impulse for self-destruction passes. We also know that the majority of suicidal people don't really want to die, they just want their pain to end. Each human life is special, and worth preserving.

Preventing teen suicide involves many different things: helping a friend on a one-to-one basis, helping to educate groups of people, helping yourself when you are feeling depressed. The first step in preventing suicide is recognizing the warning signs in a friend or yourself, and teaching others to do the same.

6

Helping a Friend

It is a myth that suicide happens suddenly, without warning. It is the final, fatal step that caps a long series of problems and failures. In most cases, however, the suicidal teenager just needs someone to help her find other ways to resolve her problems and give her reasons to go on living.

Young people spend a great deal of time with friends—perhaps more than with family members. Therefore, it is often friends who will notice behavior changes and other warning signs of suicide. And it is usually a friend to whom a suicidal adolescent will turn. Young people may feel that another person their own age will take them more seriously than an adult will, and will understand the nature of their problems.

You may hesitate to get involved because you are not an expert, but experts aren't the ones teenagers usually turn to. You are. And you can save lives by learning a few basic facts about suicide.

Warning Signs and Risk Factors

The first step in helping prevent suicide is identifying who may be at risk. There are three general categories of warning signs: what the teenager says, what he does, and what is happening in his life. Familiarize yourself with the following specific warning signs of suicide so that you will know when to take action.

Attempts. Prior suicide attempts are powerful warning signs: more than half of those who complete suicide have made a prior attempt. This is especially true if the previous attempts were left largely untreated, dismissed as "attention getters" by parents or other adults. Even though an attempt may have seemed weak, the next attempt may result in a completed suicide, since teenagers may use more lethal methods on successive attempts.

Threats. Nearly as potent as an attempt is a threat to commit suicide. Eighty percent of those who eventually kill themselves told someone of their plans beforehand. Sometimes these threats are clear: "I want to kill myself." Other times they are not as obvious: "I'm so tired that I just want to sleep forever" or "I won't be a problem for you much longer" or "I wonder where my mother's sleeping pills are." These statements usually reflect a certain level of desperation and a sense of being cornered. If no one responds with concern, the teen may move ahead and plan exactly how he will go about killing himself.

In some cases, a suicidal teen will not express herself in words, even in subtle words. Diary entries, drawings, poems, or school essays may be veiled suicide threats.

Final arrangements. About 15 percent of suicidal teens make their intentions clear through certain actions, called "making final arrangements." They will give away jewelry, CDs, clothes, even a car—items that are valuable to them. "I won't need this anymore," a suicidal teen might say to a friend. "Please take care of this for me."

Often, a teen contemplating suicide will attempt to tie up the loose ends of relationships. She will make peace with some friends, and tell others how much they mean to her in conversations or letters.

Changes in personality or behavior. Beware if a classmate suddenly isolates herself, loses interest in her friends and activities, doesn't care about grades, suffers from drastic mood swings. A girl who once lived for field hockey and now misses practice saying she's too tired to play is depressed. A boy who had always been concerned about his appearance and now wears the same rumpled clothes for days at a time is also sending you a message.

If your friend suddenly becomes involved with other teens that you sense are also depressed or troubled, she may be telling you that she feels more connected to them. If she begins to use drugs, or starts driving recklessly or drinking too much, someone needs to investigate why. Often a young person who continuously puts herself in dangerous situations is saying that the idea of dying appeals to her on some level. Self-destructive behavior includes anorexia nervosa, self-mutilation, and sexual acting out. Any kind of preoccupation with death needs to be checked out. Look beyond the personality change and ask yourself why.

Although it may sound strange, be on the alert if a friend who has been very depressed suddenly seems quite happy. In some cases, once a teen decides to attempt suicide, he actually enjoys his last few days—he's relieved, anticipating an end to his pain, enjoying a new sense of purpose.

Ongoing depression. It may be hard to determine whether a person is depressed, since many people mask their depression. Teenagers often worry that if they tell someone how desperate they are feeling, they will not be taken seriously. Depression may be disguised as apathy and boredom, or defiance and delinquency.

Although it may be difficult to recognize, depression is not without specific symptoms. A depressed friend may have a change in sleep habits (now he sleeps all the time or not at all), a change in appetite (eating much more or much less), or suffer from physical pain (headaches, general body aches).

Some other clues are excessive anxiety, lethargy, or crying. In general, a depressed person no longer takes joy in any aspect of life. She has trouble making decisions, and finds it hard to concentrate on performing ordinary tasks, like finishing homework or making a phone call. The longer depression continues, the more dangerous it becomes.

Loss. Anyone with a recent loss, or who is facing the anniversary of a loss or a traumatic event such as rape, is at risk. Death of a loved one, divorce, breakup of a romantic relationship, an impending move to another part of the country—all are losses that may bring a teenager to the brink of suicide.

Responding to Warning Signs

Once you realize that a friend exhibits many of the warning signs, you want to intervene to avert tragedy. But how?

First, listen to him. Then, talk to him. You may think you already know how to talk and how to listen. But talking and listening to a suicidal person are very different from chatting with a nonsuicidal friend. It helps to know what to say, and what not to say. And you must know how to listen effectively.

How do you start a conversation as serious as one about suicide? Wait until you can talk without the pressure of a class bell ringing or basketball practice ready to begin. Begin by saying something like, "You seem really unhappy. I wish you would tell me what is bothering you." *Remember:* you will not give someone ideas about suicide by talking with him about it. If a friend is so troubled that the possibility of him attempting suicide occurs to you, it has already occurred to him.

Do's and don'ts. Learning the "do's" and "don'ts" of dealing with a suicidal person may mean the difference between life and death. First, here are some phrases and actions to avoid.

DON'T. . .

- ✔ criticize how your friend feels. He can't help how he feels. Telling him not to feel that way will not change anything.

- ✔ say, "You can't commit suicide!" or "You don't really mean that." That may be just what it takes to make him think, "Oh no? Just watch me!"

- ✔ remind him of the pain his suicide would cause others. Some suicidal teens want to cause pain to people they believe have hurt them.

80

✔ tell him how much luckier he is than some other people. Or how unimportant his problems are in comparison with some people's troubles. He does not feel lucky. To him, his problems are overwhelming.

✔ promise that things will be better tomorrow if you can't offer him concrete solutions to his problems. That is giving him false hope.

✔ ask, "You wouldn't commit suicide, would you?" It is clear that you are assuming he wouldn't. The question is phrased in such a way that you are not giving him a chance to talk about his suicidal feelings.

✔ leave a person alone who seems to be in a high risk situation. If he has a specific suicide plan or seems extremely depressed, stay with him until you can find a responsible adult to help him.

DO...

✔ let fear guide you. Fear will cause you to take action.

✔ listen calmly, without interrupting

✔ try to get him to describe the problem in detail in his own words. Wait for a pause, then repeat what you think the person is telling you: "So what you have said is that you . . ."

✔ believe and accept your friend's feelings. Suicidal teens feel alienated. They feel that no one understands them. Let your friend know that you understand. Say, "No wonder you are in so much pain."

✔ understand that your friend may not want to hear anything you have to say. He is so wrapped up in his own pain that he may not respond to your words. Don't be hurt. This is not a rejection of you.

✔ open up the subject of suicide if he doesn't. Ask, "Are you considering suicide?" Ask the question sincerely. He will be relieved to discuss his feelings.

✔ try to get more details. Find out how long he has felt unhappy, what specific things are troubling him, whether or not he has talked with anyone else. Ask open-ended questions so that he can express himself completely.

✔ ask him what he would want each surviving family member to understand if he were to complete suicide. That will help you to understand his motives.

✔ find out how he has handled similar situations in the past. What stopped him from committing suicide before? Is this like anything else he's experienced?

✔ assess what still matters to him. What still has value and meaning? Isn't there some source of hope and joy left?

✔ suggest alternatives. Remember, suicidal teens do not have good problem-solving skills. Help your friend to pinpoint the causes of certain problems and offer realistic and concrete options. What changes can be made that would improve things? Who can he turn to? What can he do to relieve his pain and his stress? Help him to feel more in control, because helplessness is one of the feelings that leads to suicide.

- ✔ gently remind him that problems, even very serious ones, are temporary. Suicide is permanent.

- ✔ determine how serious he is. If he has formed a suicide plan and has the means to carry it out (for instance, if he plans to shoot himself and you know that there is a gun in his home), he is at high risk. If he has been drinking or using drugs, the risk is even greater.

- ✔ request that he make an agreement with you: He will not try to kill himself until he talks to you first so that you can discuss alternatives.

- ✔ make an appointment for him to see someone who can help and offer to go with him.

- ✔ ask, "What would you like me to do to help you right now?"

- ✔ GET HELP.

Don't keep it a secret. Involve an adult immediately. What's more important: keeping his secret or saving his life? A suicidal person is like a ticking bomb. And since you wouldn't try to defuse a bomb all by yourself, you shouldn't try to deal with a suicidal person alone. You need to share the burden, and your friend needs an adult, perhaps a professional counselor, to help her arrive at alternatives to suicide. It can be anyone whom you trust will take you and your friend seriously and be able to help. Call a crisis hotline if you can't think of anyone else.

If you are not comfortable "telling" on your friend, suggest people your friend can turn to, then stay with him and *make sure that he does make contact.* He may need you to tell him whom to contact and how. He is so involved with his own pain that he can't think logically.

And remember: Your friend probably would not have opened up to you if he really wanted this to be kept a secret. In all likelihood, he is hoping that you will find someone who can help him. And while he may not be able to admit it right away, in time he will be very grateful that you were able to get him the right kind of help. Don't worry that you are overreacting. The danger lies in *not* reacting.

In the end . . .

There are limits to what any one person can do. You cannot force someone else to want to live, and you are not responsible for any friend who takes his own life. By taking the steps outlined in this chapter, you are doing as much as a friend can do. *The final decision is not yours to make.*

7

Helping the Cause

In addition to offering one-on-one help to a friend in need, there are other things you can do to help the cause of suicide prevention in general.

Things to Do in School

Posters. Put up posters listing warning signs. You'll help others learn to identify potential victims. Because teens spend so much time in school, teachers, school counselors, and classmates are likely to be the first ones to notice any potentially dangerous changes.

Assemblies. Arrange a school assembly dealing with teen suicide, or with ways of coping with stress and depression. The program might include speeches by counselors, hotline volunteers, teens who have made suicide attempts, and survivor-victims such as siblings or parents. There are also excellent films dealing with suicide that are appropriate for school assemblies. (See Resources)

In classes. Suggest that health classes include lessons on developing greater self-esteem and better problem-solving skills. Such a class might also address ways to improve relationships with family members, friends, and teachers.

Nutrition Links. Inform students and teachers about the link between nutrition and mental health problems. Young people in particular tend to have poor diets, which may contribute to depression. What types of food does your school cafeteria offer? Are the food choices nutritionally sound?

Setting an example. Encourage your peers to accept all classmates. Every person has something unique and positive to offer. Teenagers must learn to avoid ostracizing someone who seems different.

Memorial services. Urge school officials to forgo glamorous memorial services for any teenager who has died. While healthy mourning should be encouraged, elevating the dead person to hero status must be avoided. Young people cannot be encouraged to view death as a romantic alternative to a problem-plagued life. Any reference to death as a time of celebration is not appropriate.

Help Access Resources

Awareness and preparation. Check to make sure the school is prepared to deal with students who have emotional problems and may be suicidal. Are referrals made for outside professional help if that's what is needed?

Provide information. Supply the guidance office with pamphlets that describe warning signs of suicide and give phone numbers for counselors, crisis hotlines, and other helpful organizations. There are many agencies that offer help, often at no charge, to those who request it. A suicidal teen may want help but not know what resources are available or how to access them. Someone needs to connect troubled kids with people who can help.

Crisis cards. Print up wallet-size Crisis Cards that list the local phone numbers of agencies that can help anyone who is feeling suicidal. Such cards can also include warning signs of or facts about suicide. Hand the cards out in homeroom, health class, or at a related school assembly.

Help for survivors. Encourage police, medical examiners, clergy, and funeral directors in your area to pass on the names of suicide survivors to a local suicide survivors support group. This way, the group leader can contact them directly and invite them to attend a meeting.

Peer Counseling

Hotlines. Volunteer to work on a suicide hotline. If there isn't one in your area, look into starting one. Often, troubled teens turn to the telephone for help because they wish to remain anonymous.

Peer counseling in school. Form a peer counseling group after participation in a proper training program. Because teens find it easier to talk to other teens, and young people are eager to help each other, such groups have been very successful. The training program for teen counselors teaches them how to listen, how to recognize danger signs, and who to alert in a life-threatening situation.

Prevent copycat suicides. If a teen suicide does occur, copycat suicides may be prevented through swift action. Teens at risk, including close friends of the dead person and those with a history of suicidal tendencies, may be identified by peers and then contacted by trained counselors. They need to discuss the recent suicide and their own feelings.

Help Remove the Means

Get political. Write letters to your congressional representatives asking them to make it more difficult for teens to access the means to commit suicide, such as barbiturates and guns.

Give speeches. Talk to parent associations or the PTA about gun availability and access.

Circulate petitions. Petition local or state officials to build better barriers on high buildings and bridges, for example.

What Others Have Done

Here are descriptions of three different organizations that concerned people created in an attempt to help the cause.

The Samaritans. Probably the most well-known suicide intervention group is the Samaritans, founded in 1958 in London by an Episcopal minister named Chad Varah. Named for the good samaritan in the Bible who helped people in need, the Samaritans was started after a 13-year old girl in Varah's congregation completed suicide. She had gotten her first period and was frightened and confused; no one had ever explained menstruation to her. Because she was involved in a sexual relationship, she thought that this was the cause of her bleeding. Perhaps she felt she was being punished for having sex, or feared she had gotten a venereal disease. In her distress, and with no one she could turn to, she killed herself.

Despite the group's religious beginning, the Samaritans is not a church-based program. The group's purpose is to "befriend the suicidal, lonely, and despairing," and it accomplishes this via the telephone.

Trained volunteers staff the Samaritans' phone lines, ready to talk with anyone who calls because he is feeling suicidal. Calls are free, and callers remain anonymous. All information is kept confidential.

A Samaritans' volunteer helps the caller by showing sympathy and understanding. Knowing that a nearly universal feeling of suicidal people is powerlessness, the volunteer encourages the caller to think about how he can regain control of his own life and determine its direction. The Samaritans' staff is not qualified to counsel callers, but they make referrals to psychiatrists, outpatient clinics, social service agencies, or physicians when necessary.

There are currently 200 Samaritan branches in over 30 countries. The first American group opened in Boston in 1974. In 1986, the Boston Samaritans established a teen-to-teen hotline called Samariteens in response to the large number of youth suicides and the increasing realization that teens often prefer to talk to peers. Maintaining after-school and evening hours, the hotline is staffed by 40 trained teenagers. Currently, the program receives about 8,000 calls a year. Samariteens staff hope to expand the program soon to reach more teenagers in need.

SAIL (Self-Acceptance Is Life). In Chapter 3, you read Brian's story. Brian, his mother, and his sister had been very involved in the Camp Fire program. Brian had been especially close to the director's daughter, K Holland, who was the sailing instructor. After he died, she was looking through a closet and found a sailboat that he had made for her years earlier. Inspired by Brian's memory, she decided to establish a suicide awareness program for high school members of Camp Fire's horizon club.

The Oklahoma Green Country Council of Camp Fire developed the SAIL program with the help of the Mental Health Association in Tulsa, Oklahoma. SAIL presents workshops at schools, churches, and Camp Fire meetings, using panel discussions, films, role playing, and personal testimony to deliver its message. Its objectives are to help students recognize the warning signs of suicide and access community resources. The program also seeks to improve teens' coping strategies and communication with family members and others who can help during a crisis. One of SAIL's mottos is: "Suicide is a permanent solution to a temporary problem."

Within the program's first two years, 19 youths exposed to SAIL contacted Camp Fire and said that they had changed their minds about committing suicide. In 1988, suicide prevention was the Camp Fire organization's national public service project.

SAIL literature includes a letter that the program's founder wrote for Brian, her inspiration. She ended it with, "This is for Brian, my sailboat maker, who stopped dreaming of tomorrow."

Coping with a Loved One's Suicide. Coping with a Loved One's Suicide is a support group that was started in 1990 by clinical therapist Amy Metcalf for survivors of those who completed suicide. The Center for Life Management and the Parkland Medical Center in Derry, New Hampshire, co-sponsor this program. According to Ms. Metcalf, such survivors are at a higher risk themselves for suicide. "Because our agency is a suicide-prevention center," she said, "this helps meet the needs of our clients."

At free weekly meetings, members of the group talk about how they are coping with the deaths of family members. Some have recently lost children, or husbands, or sisters, while for others, many years have passed since the suicide. What bonds them is the shared loss by suicide.

Because each understands how the others feel, group members are able to offer suggestions to those who are suffering, and they are able to celebrate with those who overcome hurdles. While some meetings have themes, such as coping with the holiday season, most meetings are open to free discussion. Survivors know that the meeting will always take place, whether or not they choose to attend.

8

Helping yourself

Perhaps it is not a friend who needs help, but you. You are the one who feels that no one cares, that life is not worth living, that you must escape the pain of your daily existence. Perhaps you are not suicidal, but depressed, and searching for a way to make things better. In either case, here are answers to some questions you may have about your own troubles.

When You Are Feeling Unhappy

"When you are down," I asked a group of teenagers, "what distracts you and improves your mood?" Here are some of their answers.

Volunteering. By helping other older people in a nursing home, handicapped children, or peers who need special tutoring—your sense of purpose and self-worth gets a boost. If you aren't ready to commit to a long-term program, bake cookies for the widower down the street or pick flowers for the single mom next door. Doing nice things for other people feels good.

Getting a pet. A pet needs you, will always be happy to see you, and will return the affection you give it. If you can't have a pet because you live in an apartment or someone in your family is allergic, volunteer to help at an animal shelter or offer to walk a neighbor's pet every afternoon.

Avoiding depressed people. Seek out people you can depend on to boost your morale—a friend who has a good sense of humor, a neighbor who always looks on the bright side, a relative who is calming and positive.

Exercising. Join the local YMCA, participate in intramural sports, or just go walking or running by yourself. Exercise is a way to relax, to release energy, to make your body feel healthier. You will also feel better about your appearance after a workout, and will feel a sense of accomplishment.

Reading and writing. You may want to find a book that addresses certain problems you are having. There are books in your school or local library that deal with the stresses of being a teenager, divorce, drugs, depression, and almost any subject that might concern you. Or you may want to read an adventure book or a teen romance that will provide a healthy, temporary escape.

Several teens mentioned to me that they kept journals, or often wrote letters to people that were on their minds. The letters often ended up in the trash, but venting the feelings helped reduce stress.

Learning something new. Have you always wanted to learn how to play the guitar? Talk to the music teacher at school and ask about lessons. Maybe an older teen or retired neighbor will teach you for free. Have you often thought you'd like to learn to paint? Ask the art teacher how you should begin. Learning new things makes you feel like you are growing and changing in positive ways.

Other ideas. Although the teenagers' favorite methods for improving state of mind are listed above, they had many other ideas as well. One boy said, "I ride my street bike or do something else that I have complete control over. If I succeed, I know it is because of my skill or knowledge." Another said he feels better when he lays off the junk food and starts eating well-rounded meals. Still others offered safe "escapes" as the solution: hiking, camping, going out shopping or to an animated movie, taking a bubble bath, or napping. One girl mentioned that listening to her favorite music improved her mood; another liked to catch up on overdue phone calls with friends. "Improve your mood and your self-esteem with a haircut or a manicure," suggested one teenager. "That really helps me when I'm depressed over my boyfriend."

When You Are Feeling Suicidal

A bike ride or a nap may improve a bad mood, but it will not get rid of suicidal feelings. You should follow the advice offered by those trained in suicide prevention:

Don't panic. The severe suicidal crisis will end. There is always an answer other than suicide. You just need some help in finding that answer.

Don't isolate yourself. Get out and do things with your friends, or find a trained counselor who will listen. Keep up your interest in music or sports.

Dissect your problems. With the help of an understanding adult, try to separate your problems into clear parts. This will help you to begin to solve them. For instance, are you upset because your grades are poor? Are you failing all of your classes or just one or two? Can you speak to the teacher about an extra assignment to boost your grade or a tutor to help you understand the material better? Can you drop your college-level history course and take a more manageable one?

If you are overstressed, eliminate some of the things that are causing you the most stress. Concentrate on the things that give you the most pleasure. What do you enjoy doing? Playing sports, acting in plays, working with computers, dancing? Make time for what you enjoy.

Make lists. List all of the people who would miss you if you were gone. Do you have a special relative—an aunt, grandparent, nephew, cousin—who relies on you for phone calls, letters, or visits? List all of the positive things you have done, and all of the positive things you may do in the future. Have you helped a friend work through problems? Cheered up your grandmother when she was ill? Do you plan on becoming a parent? A teacher? An engineer? List all of the positive things about yourself. Are you a good listener? Do you have a good sense of humor? Are you patient and kind?

Talk to someone. Who do you trust? Who will listen to you without passing judgment? Will a relative, teacher, neighbor, minister, or family doctor be able to help you? If you do not want to speak to someone you know, call a nearby crisis center. (Look in the Yellow Pages under "Suicide," or dial "0" and ask the operator for a referral, or look in the back of this book.)

When you call a crisis hotline, you will talk to a trained volunteer. This is someone who is very concerned and interested in your situation but is not emotionally involved, as a relative or friend might be. You may find it easier to speak with someone anonymously. By describing your problems to someone who does not know you, you may help yourself figure out what is making you so unhappy.

The person you speak with will be able to direct you to the appropriate resources in your community. He is not trained to provide therapy. He is trained to work to get you through a suicidal crisis and to help you find the long-term help you may need.

Questions about Counseling

Often, teenagers hesitate to seek counseling because of too many unanswered questions: Will he tell my parents? Will she charge more than I can afford? Will my friends find out? I asked a number of school and family counselors to respond to these and other concerns.

When should a person get professional help? Most people who think seriously about suicide or who attempt suicide will need professional help to understand their feelings.

What will a counselor do? A counselor will try to help you understand why you are so unhappy. She will ask you what has been happening in your life. She will help you to divide what seems like a large problem into smaller parts that will be easier to solve. She will not solve the problems for you, but she will guide you, suggesting options you may not have considered.

A counselor will help you develop better problem-solving and coping skills. She will help you feel empowered, not helpless. If you are suffering from severe depression, she may refer you to a psychiatrist who will be able to prescribe drugs that will help.

What will happen to me in counseling? At first, you will feel a good deal of your stress relieved just by talking freely with someone you trust, someone who is nonjudgmental. You will stop feeling trapped when you see that you have alternatives, and realize that there are solutions to your problems. Through counseling, you may discover that you are very angry with or resentful of some of the people in your life. You may realize that changes need to be made in your relationships with family members or friends.

How could I ever open up to a total stranger? It is the counselor's job to make you feel comfortable enough to talk about your problems. Counselors are trained to be good listeners and to put their clients at ease. It may take time for you to feel completely relaxed and trusting of your counselor, however.

Some people actually find it easier to talk with a stranger. Parents and friends may be too close to your situation to offer objective help. Someone who cares about what happens to you but is not as invested in the outcome, may be a better person for you to confide in.

How does one appointment a week help? When I need to talk to someone, I want to talk right away. Most people are able to save issues until their appointment, knowing that someone they trust will listen for one hour with no interruptions. You would not have to wait until your appointment if the situation became critical, however. Your therapist would meet with you in an emergency.

Part of the counseling process involves teaching patients to handle stressful situations on their own. Talking to certain friends or family members, or writing thoughts in a journal are two ways of coping with problems between appointments.

How can I be sure that the counselor won't go to my parents or teachers and tell them what I've told her? In most cases, your counselor cannot promise you that she will never talk to your parents or teachers. This does not mean that everything you say will be shared with others. It does mean that if she feels that you are in danger, she has an obligation to help you in whatever ways she feels are necessary. The important thing is to find someone whom you trust and you feel cares about you. This way, you know that she will act in your best interests, whatever that may be.

Often, a teenager's problems are related to family issues that are best addressed in family therapy. Including family members in your counseling may be the only way to begin to solve these problems. If telling a family member that you sought counseling would put you at risk, due to an abusive situation, for example, your counselor would find a way to ensure your safety.

Will my friends find out I'm going to a counselor? The decision to inform friends would be yours. Your counselor would not tell your friends that you are in her care without your consent. She may encourage you to talk to responsible friends about some issues that have been bothering you, however. It may be in your best interest to set up a network of people you can count on for support and comfort. You may be surprised to find out that your friends were already aware that you had been feeling troubled. Depressed or suicidal teens send messages that are received by sensitive friends.

Seeing a therapist or a counselor does not have the stigma that it once did. It should not be considered any stranger than confiding in a teacher, minister, relative, or best friend. Counselors are simply trained listeners who know what resources are available to help teenagers in need.

Will the fact that I went for counseling go on any kind of permanent record? Could it affect getting into college or getting a job? The fact that you received counseling should not prevent you from getting into a college or from getting a job. If you are seeing a school counselor and the problems that you are having interfere with your school work or require that you be tested or evaluated, this information may be part of your school record. But these records are confidential. Similarly, if you are meeting with a therapist at a community mental health clinic, your records cannot be shown to anyone without your permission.

If an insurance company is paying for your treatment, however, they will also have records. Different insurance companies have different rules regarding the information in their files. You will have to ask questions of your company to determine who can access your files.

How much does therapy cost? Any counseling associated with the public school system, such as the school counselor, should be free. Most community mental health agencies will make sure that a teenager who needs counseling receives treatment. Often, there is a policy that allows patients to be charged according to their ability to pay. Private therapists who will not provide free services should be able to provide the names of community agencies that can help. In some cases, family insurance policies cover the costs. In any event, concern over payment should never stop anyone from seeking help. Even if you have no money and no access to money, you will not be turned away by most community agencies.

How does someone find the right counselor? In any town or city, there are a number of places to find counselors. Look in the Yellow Pages of your phone book under suicide or suicide prevention, mental health services, or psychiatrists. Or call a family service organization, crisis hotline center, hospital, or your family doctor for a referral. The police department, youth center, community recreation center, or YMCA may also be able to give you the name of someone who can help you. If the first place you try is not helpful, try another place. Also ask other adults who might be able to provide leads, such as a relative, minister, teacher, an older brother or sister, or an adult neighbor.

One important thing to keep in mind is that every therapist is not right for every patient. You may not find the right one the first, or even the second, time. Keep trying. Eventually you will find someone whom you can trust and with whom you feel comfortable.

Will it really help? Yes. As long as you find a counselor you can comfortably confide in and as long as you are committed to working through your problems with her, it will help you. Remember, though, just as suicidal feelings take a long time to develop, they take a long time to understand.

Part IV

Afterwards

Sometimes, despite the efforts of friends and family members, despite the conversations, the counseling, the contracts, a young person takes his own life. Left behind to suffer with grief and anger and guilt are his parents, his brothers and sisters, school teachers, and friends. It has been estimated that for every suicide, there are as many as 10 people who are closely affected by it. That means that every year, 50,000 people are left to grieve for the 5,000 15- to 24-year olds who have killed themselves. And those are just the figures for one year.

Perhaps these people—who are often called survivor/victims—are the true casualties of suicide.

9

Coping in the Aftermath of Suicide

"Certainly the pain and the problems that might drive a person to take her life do not end with the suicide," wrote Jennifer's brother in a letter about her death. "In a very real sense, for those who remain and survive the suicide, they are just beginning."

Anyone who is faced with the death of a beloved friend, brother, daughter, or grandson will feel shock, grief, and denial. But the loved ones left behind after a suicide feel the added burden of guilt, anger, confusion, and shame. Perhaps it's best described as a double burden—death, and suicide.

There are few sources of help for relatives of those who have completed suicide and even fewer for friends.

Since many teenagers are as close to their peers as to their families, friends are often intensely affected. Surviving teens need special help because of the risk of cluster, or copycat, suicide. In some cases, by counseling the survivor/friend, you are preventing the next suicide.

The Emotions

Both friends and family members experience a wide range of emotions following the suicide of a loved one. Grief is chaotic. It does not follow a pattern, as some popular books seem to suggest. Here is what survivors told me about their reactions to the suicide:

Rejection.

. . . He chose to leave me. It was not as if it was an accident.

. . . He rejected me and my offers to help him.

. . . My sister abandoned me.

Anger.

. . . I hated my sister for leaving me.

. . . I never asked to be a suicide survivor and I feel angry with my brother for making me one.

. . . I know he didn't kill himself to hurt me, but that's what ended up happening.

Shock.

. . . It all happened so suddenly. We didn't have a chance to save her.

. . . Suicide is not like cancer, or even a heart attack. There is no long illness, no preparation, no hospital visits. All of a sudden, he's dead.

. . . I never got to say good-bye.

Helplessness.

. . . It's over now. There's nothing I can do. I feel so helpless.

. . . Suicide is so frustrating because you have no chance to respond—it's like someone hanging up the phone in the middle of an argument.

Shame.

. . . People ask me what I did or whether I did it to her.

. . . Our neighbors act as if the whole family is crazy since my brother killed himself.

. . . The police asked so many questions—many of them humiliating—that it was like we were criminals.

. . . People seemed to look at our family and think, "Why? What was it about her life and her family that was so bad that she wanted to kill herself?"

Loneliness.

. . . No one called me. No one knew what to say, I guess.

. . . Even people I know well walked past me on the street without saying anything.

Guilt.

. . . Was there something I could have done to stop him?

. . . If only I had told her that I loved her more often, and had been a better parent, maybe she wouldn't have done this.

. . . Sharon told me that she was thinking about killing herself and I didn't believe her.

. . . I think I'm suffering from "survivor's guilt." I feel guilty that I'm alive and Paul is dead.

. . . It's so easy to look back and see all of the warning signs, the depression, the isolation, the drug abuse. I feel so guilty that I did not take action months ago.

. . . Dead people don't answer questions. So Paul will never be able to erase the guilt I feel. It's up to me to let it go.

Denial.

. . . I still don't believe it was suicide. I'm sure she never meant to shoot herself.

. . . There was no note. For me, that means it wasn't a suicide.

. . . I have days when I really believe that my brother didn't die, that he's coming back someday.

. . . I want to run away from everything. Just get in my car and drive away.

Relief.

. . . His pain is over and I feel kind of relieved. But then I feel guilt over my relief.

. . . For the last eight years, the whole family has suffered with Jean's suicide attempts, depression, and hospitalizations. Part of me is relieved that the whole mess is over with.

Fear.

. . . I'm afraid that I will never be able to trust anyone again.

. . . I am petrified to be alone.

. . . I read somewhere that suicidal behavior is seen in 20 percent of families where there has been a death by suicide. I worry that my family will be part of that 20 percent.

Preoccupation.

. . . Why did he do it? Why, why, why? That question runs through my head all day long.

. . . I keep dreaming that I was there to stop him from killing himself.

. . . I have dreams that I see her—that she is in her room, or downstairs watching TV.

Blame.

. . . If Brian had been hit by a drunk driver, I would have someone to blame. But Brian chose to kill himself.

. . . I blamed my parents for a long time. There's just this urge to find someone responsible, someone who you can direct your anger at.

. . . Beverly took her own life. Only she is to blame. It took me over three years to be able to say that.

Depression and suicidal urges.

. . . I couldn't even get up in the morning. I came close to losing my job due to depression. I was essentially paralyzed by it.

. . . I know how much survivors of suicide suffer. That's why I can't understand why I keep thinking about suicide myself.

. . . Once my older brother committed suicide, it seemed more real to me. It seemed like an option if things got too rough.

Low self-esteem.

. . . I felt completely worthless after Bill died. It seemed like no one else would ever love me or want to be my friend.

. . . All I could think at job interviews was, why would anyone want to hire me?

Physical Symptoms

Many survivor-victims suffer from physical symptoms that range from insomnia and migraine headaches to ulcers and heart attacks. Others have anxiety attacks and lengthy crying spells. Some turn to drugs and alcohol to dull their pain. It may be guilt that creates some of these medical problems. It may also be easier for some survivors to focus on their physical symptoms and thus avoid dealing with the emotional issues.

The Healing Process

Survivors will begin to heal when they stop thinking of themselves as passive victims. The earlier a survivor takes action, the sooner he will begin to heal. Healing does not mean forgetting, it means adjusting to the suicide and learning to live with the pain.

Healing is easiest when the relationship between the survivor and the dead person was positive. Survivors also have an easier time recovering when they feel that there was no way they could have prevented the death. On the other hand, there are a number of things that can get in the way of healing. If a survivor blames himself or others for the suicide, or blames the person who died for all his problems, he will have a hard time getting past those feelings. If he denies that there was a suicide, or decides that the suicide was a brave act, he will find it difficult to move on. Survivors who lack support from family and friends have trouble dealing with their grief. Preoccupation with turning back the clock and rescuing the suicidal person is another common stumbling block. Also, therapists have found that healing is harder for the person who discovered the suicide's body.

Conduct a proper funeral. Many family members want quick, quiet services. But this only serves to perpetuate feelings of shame, and says to others that the family is feeling disgraced.

The funeral offers the surviving family members a chance to grieve, and gives friends a chance to show support. It confronts the denial most people feel when a death occurs. The person who conducts the service should be sensitive to the needs of suicide survivors, and should avoid any reference to suicide as a sin.

Talk openly with family members. Talking about the person who died, the good memories as well as the bad ones, helps the healing process. Silence only increases the survivors' pain. In fact, if pain and grief are not expressed verbally, it is likely that they will express themselves in other ways, possibly physical or mental illness. Some families disintegrate over a suicide. Love is replaced with anger and blame. Other families come together more strongly after such a tragedy. Sharing information and emotions is often the difference between the family who falls apart and the one who bonds more tightly.

Children should be included in family conversations about the suicide, too. Sadly, too many parents believe that children should be left alone to heal, or they lie to children about the suicide in the mistaken belief that the truth might hurt them. Sometimes, in trying to protect a child from pain, parents actually cause more pain. Remember Jennifer? Her first suicide attempt came right after she learned the truth about her mother's suicide 12 years earlier. Children should be given basic, age-appropriate information.

It is important for parents to understand that a child's whole world is shaken when someone dies. He thinks that if he is good, then everything around him will be good. Now he sees that this is not true. And it frightens him. Children who are told the truth and are allowed to express their feelings in a supportive environment will be able to recover from the tragedy of suicide. Children who learn to deal with pain and build good coping skills are not likely to commit suicide themselves later on.

Keep a journal. By keeping a diary or journal, a survivor can track her progress as well as get a better understanding of the nature of her feelings. Such a journal can even include letters to the person who died.

Join a support group. Getting together on a regular basis with others who have had similar losses can help lessen the loneliness of being a suicide survivor. Talking openly about the sadness, anger, and guilt of suicide in a safe, nonjudgmental environment eases a survivor's pain. One survivor described the function of his S.O.S. (Survivors Of Suicide) group this way: "By talking about the suicide, I open up an old wound that has gotten infected. Each time we go to a meeting and clean out the wound, it feels a little better." Another man who lost two family members to suicide said, "I know that I always have that time to think and talk about my grief, so it frees up the other days of the week for the practical chores of living."

Not only do survivors feel that they are helped by attending support groups, but they feel as if they provide help as well. By comforting other group members, survivors find their own feelings of self-worth improve.

As beneficial as some support groups are, however, they are not a replacement for therapy, which offers very specialized help for survivors.

Seek professional help. Many survivors decide to talk with a professional caregiver. Survivors who continue to feel anger toward family members, who have lost interest in normal activities and friends, whose health is failing, or who are preoccupied with suicide should definitely seek help from a trained therapist. Often, survivors are reluctant to get involved in counseling, afraid it will become a lifetime commitment. But most suicide survivors just need temporary help to get through a very stressful time. Often, an entire family will decide to go to counseling together.

To find a good therapist, ask friends, clergymen and clergywomen, or your doctor for recommendations. Make an initial appointment with any who sound promising and select the one with whom you feel most comfortable.

Monitor your physical health. Eating healthy foods and getting proper exercise can make you feel less depressed. Talk to your doctor about your loss and have a complete physical examination.

Tell friends what you need. Let your friends know how they can help you. They probably want to help but are afraid of doing or saying the wrong thing. If you want someone to listen while you talk about your loss, find a good listener and tell him what you need from him.

Mark the anniversary of the death in a meaningful way. For some survivors, a ritual conducted on the anniversary of the death is very important. It marks a survivor's progress on a year-to-year basis. Some families choose to celebrate the dead teenager's birthday. Each year, Brian's sister sends her mother flowers on his birthday.

Be prepared to grieve for a long time and to suffer setbacks. As Jennifer's brother said, "Time does not heal a wound like this. Time removes you from the immediate situation, but it does not make it better. It gets different. Time has covered my wound. But when I hear a song that my sister loved, or see someone who looks like her, the wound is opened again and is almost as painful as it was the day she died."

How to Help Survivor/Victims Who Are Suffering

Perhaps you are not a survivor/victim, but you know someone who is and want to know how you can help. Suicide survivors offered me these tips to guide friends and relatives:

Don't pretend that nothing happened. Visit and phone. Choose a time that you think will be best for the bereaved, not the most convenient time for you.

116

Be brief. Don't launch into lengthy speeches. A simple, sincere, "I'm so sorry" is adequate. Sometimes a silent, heartfelt hug is the best thing you can "say."

Listen. Don't try to distract a survivor from his grief. Provide him with lots of chances to relive memories and to talk about how he is feeling now. You can help a survivor clarify his thoughts by asking questions or by repeating his own words back to him, as in, "So what you said is . . ." By letting a grieving person talk things through, you're helping him work toward putting the tragedy in perspective and getting on with life.

Offer to do errands. You might do the grocery shopping or the laundry, mow the lawn, answer the phone, or put up incoming relatives.

Don't look for a silver lining. It will not help if you say, "She's with the Lord now" or "It's for the best" or "Now her pain is over." Many survivors are not ready to hear these cliches and it minimizes the tragedy.

Share in their sadness. But don't say, "I know how you feel." You can't possibly know how someone else feels. You can, however, describe a similar event that you lived through and let the other person make comparisons if he wants to.

Write a letter. Include your favorite memories of the teenager who died. Talk about the positive ways in which she affected other lives. Tell family members how much you'll miss her and why.

Discourage blame. No living person is to blame. She killed herself.

Don't insist that the survivors should try to forget. They will never forget, nor should they. They must move on, though, and hopefully their pain will diminish over time.

Help them get help. Provide the family with the name and number of someone who runs a counseling group for suicide survivors or for parents who have lost children.

Encourage them to find ways to move beyond the tragedy. But don't try to be "Mr. Fix-It." Someone has died and there is nothing you can do to change that.

Accept the survivor's grief timetable. Don't hurry a person through a loss. It takes time to heal. Be sure you offer support for a long time, not just the days immediately following the death.

Believe in her. Let your friend know that you believe in her ability to overcome this and to choose to continue living a satisfying life. Plant a seed of hope and belief.

Discuss his progress. When you notice that the grieving person is moving forward in a positive way, mention the shifts. Be ready to leave the person alone when the time comes.

In the Months that Follow

Counselors say that between 4 and 6 months after a suicide, survivors start to feel hopeful that they will be able to go on with their lives. But a suicidal death is not something people get over. Suicide permanently changes the survivors. This is what survivors and those who wish to help them must understand.

If it can be said that any good comes from something as tragic as the death of a young person, perhaps it is the new perspective that survivors have. "Little things don't bother me anymore," Jennifer's father admitted. "The car breaking down, getting a rotten golf score, those things just aren't upsetting to me anymore. My priorities have been redefined. The death of someone you love is horrible. Nothing else comes remotely close."

Part V

Lost Potential

As the first chapters of this book show, the people behind the numbers reflect real pain. The pain of the teen who took her life, and the pain of all those who loved her. Perhaps what isn't so evident at first is that we are not only losing an 18-year-old, we are losing a future 28-year old, a future 48-year-old. We are losing a mother, a Sunday School teacher, a Cub Scout leader, a thoughtful neighbor. When an elderly person dies, she takes with her the past; when a young person dies, she takes with her the future.

10

What Did the Future Hold?

You have read the tragic stories of Michelle, Brian, and Jennifer. Here is one last story for you to consider, a story with a happier ending.

Our Final Story

In the 1880s, an Indian boy was growing up with the beliefs of his mother's religion, which combined parts of Mohammedanism and Hinduism. The use of tobacco and drugs, the eating of meat, and the drinking of wine were strictly forbidden. When he was 12 years old, the boy became curious about some of these "sins." With a young cousin, he collected cigarette butts to smoke. When the boys grew tired of picking up butts, they stole money from their servants to buy real cigarettes.

As the days passed, they stole more money and smoked more cigarettes. The boys began to feel very guilty. Not only had they disobeyed their parents, but they had disobeyed the laws of their religion as well. They were afraid to admit that they had been smoking and stealing, but they couldn't bear to go through life hiding such a secret. The two decided that suicide was the only way out of their dilemma.

After collecting poisonous dhatura seeds from the jungle, they visited a temple and prayed. In a secluded spot, they ate some of the seeds. They admitted to one another their fear that the seeds would not take effect, as well as their fear that they would. Was suicide really the only option? They debated the crucial issue for some time. Finally, they decided against eating all of the seeds, and instead went back to the temple to make a good will offering and ask forgiveness.

The boy was Mohandas Karamchand Gandhi, whom we know best as Mahatma Gandhi, the heroic symbol of passive resistance. His nonviolent movement led to dramatic changes in his native India, both spiritually and politically, and helped propel the nation toward independence. He became the conscience of his country and the world.

How different the world would be today without the contributions he made. If this peace-loving prophet had taken his life at the age of 12, what would have become of the oppressed people of India? How would the course of history have been changed?

Today, 14 young people will commit suicide. Will we lose a future president today? An Olympic gold-medalist? A devoted parent or teacher or minister?

We will never know.

Resources

American Association of Suicidology
2459 South Ash
Denver, CO 80222
(303) 692-0985

**Coping With A Loved One's Suicide
Support Group**
Nutfield Professional Park
Center for Life Management
44 Birch Street
Derry, NH 03038
(603) 432-1500, ext. 133; or (603) 434-1577

**The National Center for the Study and
Prevention of Suicide**
Washington School of Psychiatry
1610 New Hampshire Avenue, NW
Washington, DC 20009
(202) 667-3008

Samaritans/Samariteens
500 Commonwealth Avenue
Boston, MA 02215
(617) 247-0220

Suicide Information and Education Center (SIEC)
201 1615 Tenth Avenue, S. W.
Calgary, Alberta
Canada T3C OJ7
(403) 245-3900

Suicide Prevention and Crisis Center of San Mateo County
1811 Trousdale Drive
Burlingame, California 94010
(415) 692-6662

SAIL Program
Green Country Council of Camp Fire
5155 East 51st Street
Suite 100
Tulsa, Oklahoma 74135-7445
(918) 663-3443

Youth Suicide Prevention Center
P.O. Box 844
Bothell, WA 98011
(206) 481-0560

Further Reading

Berman, Alan L. and David A. Jobes. *Adolescent Suicide: Assessment and Intervention.* Washington, D.C.: American Psychological Association, 1991.

Chiles, John, M.D. *Teenage Depression and Suicide.* New York: Chelsea House Publishers, 1986.

Dolce, Laura. *Suicide.* Chelsea House Publishers. New York. 1992.

Gardner, Sandra, with Gary Rosenberg, M.D. *Teenage Suicide.* Englewood Cliffs, NJ: Julian Messner, 1985, 1990.

Kolehmainen, Janet, and Sandra Handwerk. *Teen Suicide.* Minneapolis: Lerner Publications Co., 1986.

Lukas, Christopher, and Harry M. Seiden, Ph.D. *Silent Grief: Living in the Wake of Suicide.* New York: Charles Scribner's Sons, 1987.

McCoy, Kathy. *The Teenage Survival Guide.* New York, Simon and Schuster, 1981.

Schleifer, Jay. *Everything You Need to Know About Teen Suicide.* New York: The Rosen Publishing Group, Inc., 1988.

Smith, Judie. *Drugs & Suicide.* New York: The Rosen Publishing Group, Inc., 1992.

Index

A

abuse, physical, emotional, sexual, 53
alcohol and drug abuse, 54
    in the family, 54
Anne's case history, 65-68
anxiety, 40

B

Brian's case history, 29-35

C

case histories
    Anne's, 65-68
    Brian's, 29-35
    Eleanor's, 62-65
    Jennifer's, 45-51
    Michelle's, 7-13
cluster suicides, 21-22
    Bergenfield, NJ response to, 22
    The Sorrows of Young Werther, 21
competition, 24, 61
coping skills, lack of, 39-40
Coping with a Loved One's Suicide, 92
copycat suicides. *See* cluster suicides.
counseling, questions about, 98-104
culture and suicide, 24-25
    during Middle Ages, 25
    Eskimos, 25
    Japan, 23-24

D

depression, 12, 38-39, 54-55
    counseling and, 98-104
    family history and, 54-55
    self-help and, 93-96
    suicidal feelings and, 96-98
divorce, 57-58
drug and alcohol abuse, 37-38

E

Eleanor's case history, 62-65

F

families at risk, 51
family and suicide, 44

family and teenagers, 51
    alcoholism and drug abuse, 54
    depression in the, 54-55
    divorce, 57-58
    fairy tale family, 56-57
    family scapegoat, 58-59
    lack of communication, 59
    life style changes, 61-68
    mattering, 52-53
    physical, emotional, and sexual
        abuse, 53
    unrealistic expectations, 55-56
family life, changes in, 61-68
female suicide, 18
funerals, *See* memorial services.

G

Gandhi, Mohandras Karamchand,
    121-123

H

hara-kiri (seppuku), 23

I

incomplete suicides. *See* suicide attempts.
indirect suicide, 20-21
individuals at risk, 35
intervention groups
    Coping with a Loved One's
        Suicide, 92
    SAIL (Self-Acceptance Is Life), 90-92
    Samaritans/Samariteens, 89-90

J

Japan and suicide, 23-24
Jennifer's case history, 45-51

L

lack of communication, 59
    family, 59
loss, 36-37

M

Mahatma Gandhi, 122-123
male suicide, 18

Michelle's case history, 7-13
minority suicide, 19
media, and suicide
    death, real and make-believe, 72
    news reports, 71-72
    television's unreality, 73
    use in prevention, 73
memorial services, 86, 112

P

peer counseling, 88
pressures on teens
    drugs and, 70
    peer pressure and, 69-70
    technological changes and, 68-69

R

reasons for suicide
    anxiety as, 40
    attention as, 42
    control as, 41
    depression as, 12, 38-39
    drug and alcohol abuse as, 37-38
    lack of coping skills as, 39-40
    loss as, 36-37
    low self-esteem as, 12
    overreaction as, 40
    revenge as, 41
    Romeo and Juliet as, 41-42
    starting over as, 43
resources about suicide, 87-92, 124
russian roulette, 21

S

SAIL (Self-Acceptance is Life), 90-92
Samaritans/ Samariteens, 89-90
self-destructive behavior, chronic, 20-21
self-esteem, low
    and suicide, 12
self-help, 93-104
self-worth, 52-53, 56
    See also self-esteem.
social changes and suicide, 61-73
society and suicide, 60-61, 68-73

suicidal individual
    feelings of, 27-29
    helping the, 79-84
suicidal thoughts, 20
suicide
    definition of, 14-15
    differences between male and
        female, 18
    means of, 16
    minorities, 19
    statistics of, 15-16, 17-19
    stigma of and laws against, 24-25
suicide attempts, 16-17, 76-77
suicide gestures, 16-17
suicide prevention, 74
    copycat suicides and, 88
    do's and don'ts of, 80-84
    hotlines for, 88
    peer counseling and, 88
    remove the means, 88-89
    school projects, 85-86, 87
suicide survivors
    dealing with loss, 111-116
    emotions of, 107-111
    healing of, 111-116, 118-119
    physical symptoms of, 111
    ways to help, 116-118
survivor/victims. *See* suicide survivors.

T

technology, effects of, 70

W

warning signs
    attempts as, 76
    changes in personality or behavior,
        77-78
    depression as, 78-79
    final arrangements as, 77
    loss as, 79
    responding to, 79-84
    threats as, 76-77
worldwide, problems of suicide, 23